under

Three Flags

under Three Flags

BY STEPHEN NEILL

FRIENDSHIP PRESS   NEW YORK

Contents

1

Learning Independence

WORLD ISSUES AND SOUTHERN ASIA

"Out of all the people in the world, one in five is one of us." So wrote an Indian writer some years ago, and it was true. If the population of the world could be evenly redistributed, one in five of the people you meet in the street, one in five of the people you watch a ball game with, would be an Indian, a Pakistani, or a Ceylonese. More than half the people in the world live in Asia. A quarter live in southern and southeastern Asia, that belt of countries that stretches from Pakistan in the northwest to the Philippine Republic. One in five is a citizen of one of the three countries that are the subject of this book. By sheer weight of numbers, the peoples of these countries demand the interest of other human beings.

There are other reasons that make a study of these countries especially interesting and relevant at the present time.

Whether we like it or not, the division of large parts of the world between the free peoples and the Communist controlled countries, with the possibility of conflict between these two blocs, is the most pressing reality of our time. Which way will southern Asia go? The capture of China by the Communists has upset the balance of the whole world. China has overrun Tibet and now has a long common frontier with India. The free peoples are fighting exhausting wars in Indochina and Malaya; if either of these two bastions were to fall to the Communists, the whole strategic situation would be altered in the Indian Ocean, as far as Australia and New Zealand. Even the most shortsighted can see that the decisions taken in the next few years in that part of the world will have the gravest significance for North America and the whole of the West.

It is not really possible that the world should long continue one half slave and one half free. It is now equally evident that the world cannot long continue in peace if one half of it is rich and one half is poor. The poverty of the Asian countries is a world problem. Asia is poor today, as poor as western Europe was five hundred years ago, before Renaissance, Reformation, agricultural and industrial revolutions together created the modern world we know. The people of those lands are beginning to understand that there is no reason why they should remain forever poor; they are demanding that economic equality without which political equality cannot convey more than formal freedom. Western statesmanship is challenged to take up its responsibility for helping the peoples of the underdeveloped countries to a fuller and richer life.

Since the end of the war, six great independent nations have come into being in the region of which we are speaking—India, Pakistan, Ceylon, Burma, Indonesia, and the

Republic of the Philippines. Such an event has never before taken place in the history of the world. All these peoples desire to be free, democratic nations; but they are faced with the task of building up democracy without the help of that strong Christian tradition which has so profoundly influenced democracy as we know it in the West. In its new form, the democratic way of life is on trial in the world.

If Christian faith were no more than an optional occupation of pious people in their spare time, there would be no special reason why Christians as such should study contemporary history in Asia. But Christianity is far more than this. It is a maker and molder of nations. Nothing in European and American history is more fascinating than the part played by the faith in fashioning the development of national character and in shaping the growth of national life. The Christian groups in the Asian countries are tiny minorities. But insofar as they are Christian, they have hold of the great creative realities, for lack of which nations in the past have often come to disaster. Already they are playing a far greater part in the life of their nations than their numbers might suggest. Clearly it is the duty of their Christian brethren in other lands to understand their situation, to study their problems, and to help them by unfailing sympathy and prayer.

A CENTURY OF DEVELOPMENT

¶ On August 15, 1947, India and Pakistan became independent nations within the family of nations. On that day Mr. Jawaharlal Nehru, called to be the first prime minister of independent India, said:

The appointed day has come—the day appointed by destiny; and India stands forth again, after a long slumber and struggle, awake, vital, free, and independent. The turning point is past. History begins anew for us, the history which we shall live and act and others will write about.

King George VI of England, expressing the sentiments of the vast majority of his subjects, said:

Freedom-loving people everywhere will wish to share in your celebrations, for with the transfer of power by consent comes the fulfillment of a great democratic ideal to which the British and Indian peoples alike are firmly dedicated. It is inspiring to think that all this has been achieved by means of peaceful change.

At that moment a process of development, begun nearly a century before, came to its completion. British rule had started ill, with a period of disorder and even rapine. At the end of the eighteenth and the beginning of the nineteenth centuries, this had been corrected by the initiative and the actions of the great Christian governors general, Wellesley, Shore, and above all Bentinck. But still this depended on the personal character of the rulers rather than on any declared and coherent policy. The policy came in 1858, when the British Crown assumed direct responsibility for the government of India, and Queen Victoria issued her famous proclamation:

Firmly relying ourselves on the truth of Christianity and acknowledging with gratitude the solace of religion, we disclaim alike the right and the desire to impose our convictions on any of our subjects. We declare it to be our royal will and pleasure that none be in any wise favored, none molested or disquieted, by reason of their religious faith or observances, but that all alike shall enjoy the equal and impartial protection of the law. . . . And it is our further will that, so far as may be, our subjects of whatever race or creed, be freely and impartially admitted to office in our service, the duties of which they may be qualified by their education, ability, and integrity duly to discharge.

To the process set in motion by this declaration, there could be no end other than full freedom and self-government, either within or outside the British fellowship of nations. During the second half of the nineteenth century, the purpose of the Queen's proclamation was steadily implemented in a great series of measures, associating Indians ever more closely in the government of their own country.

In 1917 the goal to which all this was leading was set forth in unmistakable terms by the British Government of the day:

The policy of H.M. Government is that of increasing the association of Indians in every branch of the administration and the gradual development of self-governing institutions with a view to the progressive realization of responsible government in India as an integral part of the British Empire.

In accordance with this declaration, in 1919 the proportion of elected members in the legislative assemblies of the provinces was raised to 70 per cent, and those bodies began to function almost like the British House of Commons, except that some departments, especially Law and Order and Finance, remained directly under the control of the governor. At a later date, it was recognized that the question whether to remain within the British family of nations or to leave it was one which must be left to the free decision of the peoples of India and Ceylon.

From 1917 onward the course of development was curiously different in the three countries.

In 1928 Ceylon was provided with a constitution drawn up by a commission headed by Lord Donoughmore. No one thought that this was a very good constitution, but it opened the way for rapid development of Ceylonese initiative and responsibility, and with characteristic common sense the Ceylonese decided to accept and work it. The result was that, when independence came twenty years later, Ceylon had developed a party system and had produced a number of politicians with long experience in responsible administration. The first prime minister of independent Ceylon, Mr. Don Senanayake, had already been in office for fifteen years as an intelligent and progressive minister for Agriculture and Lands. In 1946, the constitution was revised and greatly liberalized; with some modifications this is the constitution under which Ceylon still lives. When independence came on February 4, 1948, it came without bloodshed and without dislocation either of administration or of daily life.

In India, progress was confused and sometimes distorted by the coexistence of two parallel nationalist movements.

Only history will be able to judge which of these movements rendered the greater service in this period of rapid change. The revolutionary element, the Congress Party under Mr. Gandhi and Mr. Nehru, naturally obtained far more of the limelight, as a revolutionary group always will. It is probable that, but for the efforts of this group, Indian independence would have been less rapidly won; the development through the work of

Congress of a sense of national pride and dignity was no mean contribution. On the other hand, the group that gained experience by working within the constitutional framework as it developed provided independent India with a large number of experienced politicians and administrators, without whom the transfer of power and responsibility would have been far less smooth and automatic than it actually was. By 1947 there was hardly a post that had not at one time or another been filled by an Indian and none that an Indian was not prepared to fill with competence and distinction.

The Government of India Act of 1935 provided for fully responsible government, such as is enjoyed by Australia, Canada, and New Zealand, both at the center and in the provinces of India, with certain restrictions to be applied in the event of the breakdown of constitutional government.

It was not found possible at once to bring in responsible government at the center, but in all the provinces of India government was taken over by cabinets of Indian ministers, fully responsible to popularly elected legislative assemblies. In several provinces Congress ministries came into office, and for the first time leaders of the Congress Party learned to face the problems and difficulties of government and administration on a large scale. In most cases they rose admirably to the new tasks: good progress was made especially in Madras, under the premiership of Mr. C. R. Rajagopalachari, a shrewd and high-minded Tamil Brahman, later to be the first Indian governor general of India.

When the Government of India brought India into World War II without securing the approval of the Legislative Council, all the Congress ministries resigned, without consultation with the electorate that had put them into power and without making any provision for the continuance of constitutional government. A high authority has stated that, by failing to utilize fully the provisions of the Act of 1935, Congress threw away its last chance of winning independence for a united India.

For by 1939 a new factor had entered into the situation. The Muslims began to express with no uncertain sound their demand for an independent Muslim state of Pakistan. Muslims in India numbered about a quarter of the population. In the northwest and in eastern Bengal they were in the majority; in parts of the United Provinces (now Uttar Pradesh) they were roughly equal in numbers to the Hindus; in many other areas they were a substantial minority. But, though Hindus and Muslims in many places lived together in close juxtaposition, religion served as a principle of segregation to an extent that is hardly imaginable in the West. Both Hinduism and Islam are totalitarian systems; they control the way a man thinks and the way he speaks, the clothes he wears and the way he prepares his food, his relations with his family and with his neighbors. Personal friendship between Hindu and Muslim is not uncommon, but there are many subjects that even friends find it wiser not to discuss.

Muslims had proud memories of the time when they were a conquering and a ruling people. But, as political independence drew nearer, their position seemed to worsen. Most of them were hardy fighters or sturdy tillers of the soil. They had taken to higher education in English much less readily than the Hindus, and

English education was the passport to administrative office and to political power. Full democracy, with its principle of one man, one vote, seemed to many Muslims to put them in the position of a permanent minority, with no way of insuring protection for their traditions or of exercising on the life of the country as a whole an influence proportionate to their numbers.

At first the protestations of the Muslim League, under its forceful leader Mr. Jinnah, were not taken very seriously either by the British or by the Hindus. But by 1941 it was evident that there was grave danger of a permanent breach in the unity of the country. Even as late as 1943 there was a possibility that, if Congress advocated a system of government like that of Switzerland, with a number of small units enjoying much local autonomy and with constitutional safeguards to prevent one part of the country or one religious group from tyrannizing over the rest, the Muslims might agree on the continuing unity of independent India. But Hindu national leaders had learned too well from the British and insisted on the British type of constitution, with strong control at the center and only limited autonomy for the provinces. To the Muslims, this seemed to hold out only a prospect of permanent and hopeless suppression in what would be in effect a Hindu country. Many of them would have preferred a great deal of liberty under technical subjection to the British to technical liberty with a great deal of subjection to the Hindus. By the end of the war it had become plain that there were only three possibilities before the country: the indefinite continuance of British control, civil war, or the division of the country into two separate states.

THE TRAGEDY OF PARTITION

¶ This was the agonizing situation that faced the last British governor general, Lord Mountbatten, when he reached India in 1947. There is hardly any other great area in the world that is so obviously a geographical unity. The British authorities had never even conceived the possibility of division; administration, economics, railways, even water supply had all been planned on the basis of unity. To the Hindus the unity of Mother India was more even than a conviction; it was a deep, instinctive feeling charged with passionate emotion. Yet to the Muslims separation had come to present itself as the indispensable condition of survival. Lord Mountbatten made it clear that, in the situation that then prevailed, immediate independence for India was impossible without the division of the country. Faced with this implacable dilemma, the Congress leaders decided to pay what they judged to be the lesser price, and agreed to the creation of Pakistan. That unity which was the greatest positive achievement of Britain in India was at an end.

Partition was followed by immeasurable disaster. Feelings on all sides had been grievously inflamed by agitation and propaganda. A wave of violence broke out all along the proposed frontiers of the new states, Hindus, Sikhs, and Muslims becoming involved in horrible scenes of violence, rapine, and massacre. These were accompanied by one of the greatest mass migrations in history, many millions of Hindus fleeing eastward and Muslims westward, from what may have been imaginary perils, to seek safety in the lands of their coreligionists. How many people perished in this cataclysm it has been impossible to determine. The lowest estimate is half a million, but probably three quarters of a million would be nearer the mark—more than twice the fatal casualties suffered by the British Commonwealth in six years of war.

Mercifully, the massacres did not spread to the whole of India. Within a few weeks hatred seemed to burn itself out by its own violence. Leaders on both sides exercised themselves to the full in seeking peace and the renewal of confidence. Ere long outward peace was restored, but this was a most inauspicious beginning for the life of two independent peoples. Millions of bereaved families still carry bitter memories of those dreadful days, and the two governments started life burdened with one of the gravest refugee problems in the world.

A COMMONWEALTH TRANSFORMED

¶ One of the first tasks of the three new nations was to determine their relationship to the British Commonwealth. It had been made perfectly clear that each had absolute liberty of choice and that not a finger would be lifted to stop them if they chose to leave the Commonwealth. It is one of the most remarkable facts of modern history that each of the three nations freely and voluntarily chose to remain within the British family of nations.

On January 26, 1950, a new constitution came into force in India, under which that country became a "sovereign democratic republic." The question was at once posed whether a republic could remain within a Commonwealth of which a Queen is recognized as the head. Even the British nation, accustomed as it is to performing prodigies of political versatility and accepting revolutions without noticing that they have occurred, for a moment rubbed its eyes; but the political adjustments were made quickly and without friction, and the Commonwealth transformed itself overnight to make possible the inclusion of a republic. On the Queen's birthday in 1952, the Union Jack flew over the Parliament House in Delhi side by side with the Indian flag. Objections from the parties of the left were overruled by the Speaker. The Union Jack has come to be in India what it has always been in Britain, the symbol of the greatest voluntary union of free democratic peoples that the world has yet seen. At the coronation of Queen Elizabeth II, the Prime Ministers of India and Pakistan entered Westminster Abbey side by side.

Pakistan was slow in working out its new constitutional forms. For six years it lived under a provisional constitution, and its governor general, since independence a Pakistani, was appointed by the Queen. It was only in 1953 that Pakistan decided to declare itself an independent Islamic republic within the British Commonwealth of Nations. Even now there is still much hard constitutional work to be done before the new order can be regarded as complete.

Ceylon has chosen dominion status almost exactly like that of Australia or New Zealand. At its own request, it has a British governor general appointed by the Queen, but at the next vacancy the Government of Ceylon, like that of Canada, may ask for a native born governor general.

One of the greatest living authorities on constitutional

law, Sir Ivor Jennings, vice chancellor of the University of Ceylon, has pointed out that the decisions of these countries to remain within the Commonwealth were made on the basis of a calculation of advantages to be gained and not through any sentimental attachment to Britain.

Sir Ivor enumerates as the arguments that probably weighed with the statesmen: the advantages of continued contact in the diplomatic field with the Foreign Office and the Dominions Relations Office in London, the strength that the Commonwealth can lend to any member that is exposed to armed aggression from without, the intimate commercial and financial relations that at present bind together the nations of the Commonwealth and that it would be no advantage to disrupt, and the intellectual dependence of the professional classes on the English language and particularly on the United Kingdom.[1]

In general it must be agreed that Sir Ivor is right. Yet perhaps he underestimates the strength of deeper motives. Many of the statesmen of the three nations are graduates of British universities and are passionately devoted sons of their intellectual home. When this chapter was written, the prime ministers of all the three countries were graduates of Cambridge University. Many more were educated in British mission institutions and are bound to their old teachers by that strong personal loyalty, as between teacher and pupil, that is one of the most attractive features of the age old traditions of the East. And so far there is no sign at all that any of the three nations has regretted the decision to

[1] *The Commonwealth in Asia*, 1951, pp. 116, 121-22.

stand by the other partners in a world wide democratic fellowship.

The new nations took in hand their new tasks amid the confusions left by the receding tides of war. And circumstances have not favored them in their first years of independent responsibility.

In January, 1948, Mr. Gandhi was assassinated by a young fanatic of the conservative Hindu right wing. This was a shocking and horrible crime. Yet to those who knew India from within it did not come altogether as a surprise. For nearly thirty years the passions of an emotional people had been frequently inflamed, and there had been many attempts at political assassination. Mr. Gandhi's policies and practices had challenged traditional Hinduism at vital points and were bitterly resented by conservative Hindus. Yet no words could be too strong to condemn the murder of one who had made a unique contribution to the development of modern India and was almost idolized by the masses of his fellow countrymen. There was for a moment grave danger of violent outbreaks and indiscriminate reprisals. It is greatly to the credit of the Indian people that little of the kind occurred and that, after a few days of passionate grief, the people set themselves again to the urgent tasks that were still to be done in building up the life of the new nation.

Even more serious in its possible consequences was the assassination, on October 16, 1951, of Mr. Liaqat Ali Khan, the prime minister of Pakistan. The assailant was a young Pathan from the northwest, whose motives are even now obscure. Just because Pakistan has fewer statesmen of world rank, Liaqat's death at that

moment seemed an irreparable disaster. A sober estimate
of his career tells us that:

He did not appear to be one of the Lord's anointed, if
only because he seemed to be too practical and levelheaded,
in a word, too normal a person, to rank among those who
are destined to make history or to win the martyr's crown.
Yet, by virtue of sheer solid achievement, packed into the
space of four testing, critical years, he takes his honored
place among the great ones. . . . Pakistan is his memorial and
stands for all to see. Four years ago the world as a whole
was inclined to regard her as a figment of Jinnah's brain,
an artificial creation of dubious survival value. . . . Three
years have passed [since the death of Mr. Jinnah in 1948]:
three years in which Liaqat Ali Khan's leadership has
carried Pakistan through difficulty and crisis to the achievement of a degree of political stability remarkable for a
newly formed Eastern state, of economic prosperity beyond
her own rosiest dreams, and of an honored place in the affairs of nations.[1]

Once again the crisis was surmounted with rapidity
and common sense. Khwaja Nazimuddin, governor
general since the death of Mr. Jinnah, stepped down
from that more peaceful and exalted office to take over
the arduous duties of the premiership. He had been a
minister of the government of Bengal as long ago as
1929 and had vast acquaintance with the practical world
of administration. Mr. Ghulam Mohammed moved up
from the post of finance minister to that of governor
general. In April 1953, Khwaja Nazimuddin was succeeded as prime minister by Mr. Mohammad Ali, who
at the time of his appointment was Pakistani ambassador
in Washington.

As though to ensure that none of the three nations

[1] *The Round Table*, Dec., 1951, p. 8. Used by permission.

should be exempt from tragedy, Ceylon was visited by grievous loss, when on March 21, 1952, the prime minister, Mr. Don Senanayake, was thrown from his horse during an early morning ride and died the next day without ever recovering consciousness. Senanayake was a simple man, dowered with massive common sense and unfailing geniality, who believed in the virtues of the village folk, understood them, and was understood by them. He led his country from dependence to independence without the shedding of a single drop of blood, and set her on the path of stable democratic government. After a period of doubt as to who should succeed him, the choice fell on his son, Mr. Dudley Senanayake, a graduate of Corpus Christi College, Cambridge, a "man of strong character and unswerving integrity," who, though only 40 years of age, was already serving as minister for Agriculture and Lands in his father's government. In 1953, Mr. Senanayake retired because of ill health and was succeeded by Sir John Kotelawala, yet another Cambridge graduate.

The capacity of the three nations to withstand these successive strokes of doom is evidence of the stability they have already attained. Nevertheless, they are still wrestling with grave problems, for many of which no satisfactory solution has yet been found. It may help the Western reader to sympathize intelligently with them if a brief account of a few of these problems is given.

THORNY PROBLEMS

¶ The first is that of language. In most of the nations of the earth, and most conspicuously in the United States, a common language is one of the strongest bonds of nationhood. None of the new nations in southern Asia has a common language.

In Ceylon, the two main languages are Singhalese and Tamil, which are mutually unintelligible. For a century the language of common intercourse between educated men has been English. Under the influence of national sentiment, there is a strong move to develop the two indigenous languages and to insist that every pupil in the schools must be educated in the language of the group to which ethnically he belongs. But, in spite of some attempts to set up Singhalese, the language of the majority, as the national language of Ceylon, attempts that are certain to be strenuously resisted by the Tamil community, the new emphasis on the local languages may have the paradoxical result of laying yet greater emphasis on English as the sole common medium of communication.

In West Pakistan the principal language is Urdu, that elegant hybrid that came into existence in the fifteenth century, when the soldiers and nobles of the Mogul armies imposed a mainly Arabic and Persian vocabulary on a grammatical structure derived from the ancient languages of India. But in East Pakistan the immense majority speaks Bengali, one of the most musical and best developed of Indian languages, and one of the few that has a considerable and meritorious modern literature. It has been laid down that ultimately Urdu must be the official language of the whole of Pakistan.

Early in 1952 mischief-makers sedulously spread it abroad in East Pakistan that from April 1 people would be forbidden to speak Bengali even in their own homes; students were told that, as they were not qualified in

Urdu, there would be no jobs for them, and clerks in government employ who did not know Urdu were made to believe that they would be dismissed forthwith. The result was serious rioting in Dacca, in which a considerable number of people were killed. It was not long before order was restored, and the Chief Minister moved in the Assembly a resolution that Bengali should be adopted as a second official language on an equal footing with Urdu; but the events of those terrible five days have revived in many minds old doubts as to whether Pakistan is really viable as a single modern state.

In India the situation is even more complicated. The great Linguistic Survey carried out by the British Administration lists 220 languages apart from dialects. Even when all the smaller groups have been excluded, there are at least fifteen main languages, each spoken by many millions of people. The four great Dravidian languages in the south are of completely different structure from those of the north, though there is a certain similarity in vocabulary. The aim of the state is that in fifteen years' time from the attainment of independence Hindi shall be the official language of the whole country. Hindi is the language of a large number of people in North India, but it is of comparatively recent development and its literature is not to be compared with those of Tamil and Bengali. The process of adapting it to all the purposes of modern science and industry has only been begun.

In most schools, instruction is now given in the "mother tongue" (regional language), with pressure to adopt Hindi as the second language, English coming only third. Some schools have obtained permission to reintroduce English as the medium of instruction. The leading Christian paper in South India complains: "The result is that at the fourth or fifth form stage, there is a considerable trek . . . from the mother tongue medium schools to the English medium schools." [1]

Another thorny problem concerns the prohibition of alcoholic liquor. High caste Hindus disapprove the use of alcohol, and the Congress Party came into power pledged to introduce total prohibition. Many large areas, such as Madras State with a population of fifty million, have gone completely "dry." Christian opinion in the main supports Congress policy in this matter. It is affirmed that beneficent results have already become apparent in the reduction of debt, increased savings, and better health, since money formerly spent on drink is now spent on food. In one village not far from Bombay it was found that twenty families of potters and fifteen other families had cleared their debts and were now living happily, one man having amassed a fortune of Rs. 2400 since prohibition came in and another who was formerly constantly in debt being now the owner of five acres of land.

Many Indians, however, take a less optimistic view of the situation. Madras, in introducing prohibition, gave up revenue of seventeen crores of rupees (more than $30 million), at a time when every available rupee was needed for nation building activities. A large special force had to be employed in the detection of offenses against the prohibition laws. The jails have had to be enlarged, since at one moment in 1951 as many people

[1] *The Guardian* (Madras), July 17, 1952, pp. 226-27.

were in prison in Madras State for prohibition offences as in Great Britain, a country of roughly equal population, for all offenses of every kind.

It is by no means certain that the result of all this has been a decrease in drinking. An official committee of inquiry in Madhya Pradesh reports that prohibition has failed, since public support for it is lacking and there is too much collusion of the lower ranks of the police and the excise department with illicit distillers. So far the Congress Party has seen no reason to change its policy, believing that by patient persistence it can change the habits of the people; but it is certain that in the future much will be heard of this intractable problem.

Other problems have grown out of the disposition of territories ruled by Indian princes. Under the British, two fifths of the area of the Indian subcontinent was ruled by these princes, each of whom was protected in his rights by a separate treaty. With separation and independence it was arranged that the princes with their territories should accede to one or the other of the new dominions. It was one of the greatest triumphs of the new order that almost all the princes peacefully acceded to that dominion within which their territories were situated and accepted an arrangement that offered them dignity and opportunities of usefulness, without the independent authority that they had enjoyed in earlier years.

In certain cases, however, difficulties arose. The ruler of the greatest state of all, the Nizam of Hyderabad, with a territory almost equal in size to Great Britain and a population of about sixteen million, refused to sign an instrument of accession to either dominion, though he was prepared to make a treaty with both, and claimed the right to be an independent sovereign. India refused to admit the Nizam's right to independence and sent an army to invade the state. The campaign was brief, and after a few days the Nizam capitulated.

By far the most serious of the contemporary problems is the tension between India and Pakistan on the subject of Kashmir.

The state of Jammu and Kashmir in the far northwest of India consists of three parts: the lovely vale of Kashmir itself, where the population is mainly Muslim; provinces on the south and east of the Pir Panjal range of mountains, which are mainly Hindu; and an immense extension of territory to the east and north, far into Central Asia, where the people are Tibetan in type and Buddhist by religion. Both India and Pakistan have natural interests in the region, Pakistan because Kashmir controls the headwaters of three of the great rivers that are her very lifeblood and India because Kashmir has a common frontier many hundreds of miles in length with Turkistan and Tibet. With the rapid advance of communism into these lands, Kashmir is bound to play a vital part in the defense policy of the Indian peoples.

In Kashmir, though the great majority of the people are Muslim, the ruler was a Hindu. He signed an instrument of accession to India, and Kashmir became part of the Indian dominion. Pakistan objected, on the ground that the views of a ruler, descended from a family arbitrarily imposed upon Kashmir by the British little more than a century ago, ought not to be allowed to determine the fate of his subjects without consultation with them.

Situations will not always wait for the deliberations of statesmen. Tribesmen from the northwest invaded Kashmir, helped by Pakistani troops; India was able to rush in an army just in time to defend Srinagar, the capital. The territory was divided, and the division was maintained by the occupying armies. India was irritated by the failure of the West to accept what, from the Indian point of view, was a cast iron legal case. Pakistan felt itself betrayed by the failure of the West to intervene in what to it appeared as a clear violation of justice in the name of law. The dispute came very near to involving two great nations in war. For nothing less than that was involved. During August, 1951, 90 per cent of the Indian armed forces were massed on the Pakistan border.

From the beginning of the Kashmir dispute in 1947, the governments of India and Pakistan had agreed that the future of the 84,000 square mile state should be decided eventually by a plebiscite of its four million inhabitants. In the interim between the end of military conflict and agreement upon a neutral administrator for the plebiscite, the state remained divided by a cease fire line policed by a mixed team of United Nations observers. But by the end of 1953, the two nations had not yet been able to agree on the conditions under which the plebiscite should be held.

Kashmir is only symptomatic of something much deeper, the way in which India and Pakistan have as it were turned their backs on each other. Psychologically the impact of division on the two parts of the subcontinent was very different. To India, partition was a horrible thing, accepted for the moment from sheer necessity but never acquiesced in. Almost all Indians in their hearts dream of the restoration of the lost unity. To Pakistan, partition came as relief and deliverance; it presented both the challenge and the opportunity of building up a new free life, unhampered by the penetrative influences of Hinduism. The eyes of India are directed mainly east and north, to Indonesia and China and beyond. Pakistan turns west and, very conscious of its new status as the largest of the Islamic states, looks to the world wide brotherhood of Islam for support. However much it may be regretted, partition with all its consequences, political, economic, and religious, must be accepted as a permanent fact in the world situation; to imagine otherwise is only to foster illusion. Since Mr. Mohammad Ali became prime minister, relations between the two countries have greatly improved and are now more hopeful than at any time since 1947. In July, 1953, Mr. Nehru visited Karachi, the capital of Pakistan, and was enthusiastically welcomed by the populace.

In one respect the policies of the two countries are likely to coincide. Both are determined to maintain the principle of Asia for the Asians. Both are conscious of all that release from the thralldom of the West has meant to them. Both can be counted on to support any movement of "colonial" peoples in Asia or elsewhere for independence and to oppose what they regard as imperialism.

For this reason both are likely to maintain what to those in the West may seem a perplexing attitude of detachment from both the American and the Russian ideals and ways of life. Viewed from Asia, there really is not much difference between the two. Both Russia and the United States call themselves democracies; Russia has the advantage of better treatment for the colored races; the United States has the advantage of better preservation of individual liberty, but in the East individual liberty is a new idea much less ardently treasured than in the West. To Indians, the Russian and the American ways of life are only variants in detail on the common theme of Western materialism. Both seem to make material production their god and cast out all those spiritual factors that make life worth living.

Every educated Indian is conscious of belonging to a civilization far older than those of the West, with a continuous spiritual tradition running back at least three thousand years. His principal aim is to avoid becoming entangled with either the Russian or the American system and to have space, geographical and spiritual, in which to work out his own third way, in which the dominance of the spiritual can be reconciled with better provision for the everyday needs of men.

Whether in the agonies of the mid-twentieth century such a third way can be found may be questioned. It is important that Americans should take seriously this Indian search. Otherwise they will fail to understand the apparent vacillations of Asian foreign policy and are likely to be irritated by the failure of the Asian powers to take a firm stand on the side of what the West has identified with the cause of democracy and civilization.

PROGRESS IN SELF-GOVERNMENT

¶ The enumeration of difficulties and problems must not be allowed to obscure the greater reality that in six years the peoples of all the three countries have made outstanding progress in the understanding and exercise of democratic self-government. This affirmation is based not only on general impressions but in particular on the experiences of the elections held in 1952 in Ceylon and in India.

In Ceylon, the election resulted in an overwhelming triumph for the National Party, which returned to power with a large majority over all the other parties combined. The Communist-dominated parties won only thirteen seats in a house of 101 members.

Ceylon is not as peaceful politically as these figures would suggest. Its outstanding problem is the status and rights of the large number of Indian residents of Ceylon. In earlier days, the whole Commonwealth enjoyed common citizenship. As a result of recent constitutional changes, this no longer applies, and citizenship has to be locally acquired, a development that flatters the national pride of the dominions but involves a considerable number of inconveniences.

The terms laid down for the acquisition of citizenship in Ceylon did not commend themselves to a number of the Indian residents; many of them applied too late and were therefore unable to acquire rights as voters. In consequence, the Ceylon Indian Congress as a whole took no part in the elections. This is a serious matter; discontent in the large Indian minority and a sharp division between the Singhalese and the Tamils would gravely threaten the unity of Ceylon, at a time when internal unity is especially necessary in face of disruptive influences that may threaten from without.

The Indian elections, which took place in the early months of 1952, were an astonishing achievement. The new constitution had brought in adult suffrage for both sexes. This meant that an electorate of 176 million voters had to choose more than 700 members for the two houses of the central government and 3,278 members of assemblies in the states. Critics of India were frankly sceptical; even her warmest friends were doubtful as to what would happen in so gigantic a test. The final figures show that over 107 million people went to the polls. It is clear that the method of having on the voting cards clearly recognizable symbols for each of the political parties worked well, so that even illiterate people knew what they were doing and recorded their votes according to their convictions. This memorable triumph of democratic method and principle reflects the greatest possible credit on all concerned and on the Indian people as a whole.

The results, when analysed, are rather disturbing. Congress, the party of Mr. Nehru and his supporters, was returned with a large majority of seats at the center and in most of the states. But it returned as a minority party. In the state elections, it polled 43 million votes, as against 60 million cast against it. It was saved only by the many divisions among opponents and the failure of any single alternative party of opposition to appear. The purely communal parties, such as the very conservative Hindu Mahasabha, suffered resounding defeat. But the Communists arrived as the second party in the state, having won 23 places in the House of the People at the center and 181 seats in the various assemblies. The nature of these Communist successes demands somewhat careful analysis.

It is often stated that misery naturally breeds communism, and that, in view of the economic misery of the Indian people, it is natural that they should turn to communism. The facts of the Indian situation hardly bear out this generalization. It is to be noted that not one of the Communist leaders is either a worker or a peasant; all are intellectuals. Not a single Communist was returned from any of the great centers of Indian industrial life and none from the areas where drought and famine had pressed most hardly on the people. The largest Communist vote was in Travancore in the southwest, where the percentage of literacy is the highest in India. It is evident that many Christians voted Communist.

Part of the reaction against Congress was simply the normal reaction against a government that had been in power for more than four years and had governed through a period of great stress and difficulty. But there was more in it than this; there was an increasing doubt in the minds of many as to whether Congress was a genuinely popular party, able and willing to govern in the interests of the common man, the underdog, or whether it was simply an alliance between the intelligentsia and the Indian capitalists to maintain the traditions of bourgeois domination. An accurate observer, who knows India well, tells us that, especially in the south, "Communists are recruited among the ablest and most upright students; it seems to them that the Communists alone concern themselves with the needs of the great mass of the people. Others, children of privileged families, utterly disheartened by the selfishness they see all around them, look to communism for a program of social and economic equality; they feel the need to give themselves to a great cause." [1]

A careful analysis, published by the National Christian Council of India, suggests the following reasons for Communist success:

A lack of personal integrity in former Congress representatives. This, coupled with a pride which separated them from the people they represented, cost Congress more votes than any other one cause. Corruption had gotten out of hand. . . . Unfulfilled political promises to the Harijan [outcaste] community and the laboring classes widened the gap between the "haves" and the "have-nots" until the Harijan community lost all faith in Congress. . . .

In many districts police repression was vividly remembered and resented. Despite repeated denials by the authorities, in 48/49 . . . repression was exceedingly severe and at times brutal . . . excellent fuel for Communist propaganda, although their share in causing the violence is conveniently forgotten. . . .

The Communist worker has a missionary zeal. . . . They observe no caste distinction and put their sympathy for the Harijan into open practice.

The imagination of students in high schools and colleges . . . was captured. [2]

No one can estimate exactly the extent of Communist penetration. There is no doubt that propaganda is ceaseless, intelligent, and appealing. On a railway bookstall in South India it is possible to buy for 25 cents a five hundred page work on communism, well printed and bound, which must have cost at least ten times that amount to produce. Books in large quantities are sent in free from Russia. It has been stated that the bookseller

[1] Roger Hicks in *Nouvelles de Caux*, April, 1952.
[2] *The National Christian Council Review*, May, 1952, pp. 228-29. Used by permission.

gets 40 per cent of the retail price, while 60 per cent goes to the funds of the Communist Party in India, a neat way of at the same time spreading doctrine and unobtrusively financing the party.[1]

It is evident that in India poverty as such plays only a small part in the spread of Marxist ideas. Two causes are predominant. The first is the inability of the present government, which was so lavish of promises before it came to power, to fulfill its promises and bring in an era of prosperity and happiness. The other is disgust at the incompetence and corruption that is daily more evident, after a long period of occasionally unsympathetic but extraordinarily efficient administration under the British. Complaints about the spread of corruption are heard not only from those who suffer under it, but in official statements by the government itself. In the fight against the spread of communism, American Point Four aid will help. But the primary need is for good, honest, upright, efficient government. The urgent question is as to which, if any, of the existing political parties can supply such government.

In India, as in North America or Europe, all political and economic problems have eventually to be interpreted in the light of the moral and the spiritual. This is where the challenge to the Christian, and his opportunity, come in. Neither Hinduism nor Gandhian idealism has been able to supply moral fiber and missionary enthusiasm on the scale required to meet the needs of contemporary India and to create a real hope for the

---

[1] "The Lessons of the Elections in India," by E. Stanley Jones, in *National Christian Council Review*, May 1952, p. 237. Used by permission.

future in place of the illusory hopes that communism offers. Can the Christian gospel do any better? The answer to this question depends on the moral caliber of the Indian Christians now engaged in political life and government service and on the quality of life manifest in the Christian communities. And that depends on the extent to which the transforming power of the risen Christ is unmistakably manifest in his church in India, Pakistan, and Ceylon.

2

Fighting Poverty

A stay of twenty-four hours in India or Pakistan is enough to assure the visitor that these are impoverished countries. The situation is better in Ceylon, but even there the general standard of living is lower than would be acceptable anywhere in western Europe or America. This is undoubted fact. Yet it is not easy to speak constructively or with complete accuracy of Indian poverty.

Unfortunately the majority of American visitors to India make their first contacts in Bombay or Calcutta. The horror they experience in the slums of those vast and overcrowded cities is like that felt by the Indian visitor to America when confronted with the slums of Harlem or the south side of Chicago, except that the Indian feels that the slums of the United States, the richest country in the world, are much less excusable than those in his own land. But Bombay and Calcutta, especially in the terribly exaggerated overcrowding of the post-partition period, are not typical of India; their bitter poverty must be balanced by seeing the solid though modest comfort of, for instance, a village of Jats in the north or Reddies in the south.

It does not help to set out India's poverty in terms of dollars and cents. Although the cost of living has quadrupled itself since 1939 and money does not go nearly so far as it used to, it still goes a great deal further in Asia than it does in America; to translate the average earnings of the Indian peasant or worker into dollars and cents and to compare it with average earnings in the United States is wholly misleading in terms of purchasing power.

It is well not to use the word "misery" too often; this suggests that folk in Asian countries spend their time being miserable, and this is most unfair to the vigor, courage, and almost unfailing cheerfulness of a great people. No one who has seen the young men of a South Indian village playing games in the streets far into the night under the full moon can doubt their immense capacity for enjoyment. A sympathetic observer was inclined to pity the women in the cotton picking season. She found to her surprise that the women greatly enjoyed this time; the work is extremely hard and taxing, but the long hours in the bright sparkling air under the glorious South Indian sky, and the pleasant, friendly evenings and nights, spent in the open air or in temporary shelters, are health giving, and play in their lives much the same part as the jaded New Yorker's holiday in Maine or the Laurentians. Even the children who spend long and lonely days pasturing the cattle on the scanty grass of the wastelands have innumerable games that they play among themselves and find the hours pass slowly but not unpleasantly away.

It is a mistake to imagine that the whole population of the Indian subcontinent is hungry and undernourished all the time. The outcastes have the very worst of it; yet in many areas sturdy families follow the harvest from farm to farm across the plains, and in the four months' work of the two harvests collect as payment enough grain to keep them comfortably fed for eight months of the year.

Yet when we have said all that can be said in mitigation, it remains a fact that Indian poverty is terrible. A part of the population is hungry nearly all the time. A larger part is undernourished for two or three months every year. A still larger part lives very near the poverty line. One bad season produces grave hardship; failure of the monsoon rains in two or three successive years is likely to result in famine and actual starvation.

India, still mainly a land of primitive agriculture, is dangerously dependent on its rainfall. There has perhaps never been a year in which the rains have failed over the whole subcontinent, but through the centuries famine has been a recurrent terror. Earlier rulers, Indian or British, looked on with anguish but with a feeling of helplessness. The overwhelming difficulty was that of transport. India's commerce, which made her capitalists as rich as any industrial magnates in the world, was almost entirely in small light objects—silks, spices, and jewelry, which could easily be moved and which brought in enormous profits when carried to the West. Grain is bulky and heavy. When the only method of transport was the bullock cart, moving placidly at two or three miles an hour, or the pack horse or camel, grain could not be moved quickly enough or in large enough quantity from the prosperous areas to those in dire need.

The railway came as the savior of India; her first great charter of freedom from want was Lord Dalhousie's memorandum of 1854 on the development of the railway system. Railways were rapidly developed by the government, and on strategic lines, not only for the defense of the country from outside enemies but still more for defense against famine. The traveler today sometimes wonders at the long loops and detours of the railway; he may not realize that these routes were deliberately planned to carry the lines through areas of defective rainfall and to make possible the rapid movement of grain.

In 1880 the British administration set forth its incomparable Famine Code. Every civil servant was trained in this code. Every year detailed information on the rainfall and the state of crops had to be sent into headquarters; at the first sign of scarcity, machinery was set in motion to deal with it. If famine threatened, grain was rushed in from richer areas and distributed under government control, relief works were set up to keep the people from being dependent on mere charity, and steps were taken to guard against the epidemics that almost always accompany famine. After the crisis had passed, the peasants were helped by remission of taxation and the distribution of seed, free or at reduced rates, to help them start again the work of the farms. So successful was this skilled handling of the problem that between the great famine in South India in 1877, vividly described by Rudyard Kipling in one of the best of his Indian stories, *William the Conqueror,* and the Bengal famine of 1943, induced by the wholly abnormal conditions of the war period, there was only one large scale famine in India.

But prevention is better than cure. Dams and irrigation can guard against failure of the rains and immensely increase the cultivable area of a country. This was well known to the ancient rulers of India; their successors were quick to see and to exploit the possibilities. The great rivers of the northwest, the "five rivers" that water the Punjab, were flowing largely unused to the sea. They had cut out deep channels, far below the surrounding country, and between them lay great tracts of unattractive scrub and jungle country, beloved only of the hunter, since they were the haunt of the wild boar and other game. Successively all these rivers have been harnessed by mighty dams and forced by modern engineering skill to yield to the farmer their incalculable riches.

The Sukkur Barrage on the Indus, opened in 1932, feeds 6,816 miles of canals, and has added three million acres to the cultivable lands of India. Almost every year saw some great addition to the network. In South India, the Periyar was caused to flow back through the mountains and to discharge part of its waters into the Bay of Bengal instead of into the Arabian Sea. By the end of the British period, 32½ million acres of previously unused land had been added to the fruitful fields of India; millions of people had been given new hope and a quite new level of prosperity. "These canals have done much more than safeguard areas of doubtful rainfall from famine; they have caused millions of acres of rainless wasteland to blossom like the rose. Canal colonies, with their robust, prosperous, and forward looking inhabitants, are now a regular feature of Indian life." [1]

A third step in the direction of prosperity was the opening up of the hill areas for the growth of tea, coffee, and rubber. Hundreds of thousands of acres of jungle were cleared. In 1949, the record year, India exported 265,000 metric tons of tea. These plantations, built up at first by European energy and capital but now largely in Indian or Ceylonese hands, have brought wealth to unproductive areas, have afforded an invaluable area of alternative work for the peasants in times of scarcity, and have assured to hundreds of thousands of permanent workers a stable and reasonably high level of economic prosperity.

The fourth phase of the assault on poverty was industrialization. Until well on in the twentieth century, British administration in India took little part in planning or developing industries. Nevertheless, in the eighty years before the second world war, India rose from being an almost wholly agricultural country to the eighth place among the manufacturing nations of the world. Much of the enterprise was British or Swiss. But the famous Parsi firm of J. N. Tata created at Jamshedpur one of the largest iron and steel industries in the world, and, as a side line, built up Air India, one of the most efficient and reliable of airlines.

Some of the industrial developments, such as those that have resulted in the horrible overcrowding of Bombay, have been deplorable. But not all are of this kind; Messrs. Harvey's spinning mill at Papanasam in South

[1] *India, Pakistan and the West*, by Percival Spear, p. 171. London, Oxford University Press, 1949. Used by permission.

India, at one time reckoned the largest spinning mill in the world, was built in entrancing scenery at the foot of the southern Ghats, the water power from which was used for the purposes of the mill; conditions of work are admirable, and most of the thousands of workers live in their own villages round about, balancing the necessarily somewhat artificial life of a great industrial plant with the immemorial traditions of the Indian village.

By the end of the nineteenth century, these combined attacks on want were beginning to show measurable effects; the first quarter of the twentieth was a time of steady though unsensational progress. The capital wealth of the country in roads, railways, bridges, and factories was steadily expanding. Millions of tons of additional food were being grown every year. The increased prosperity of the people was manifest in the substitution of tiles for the traditional thatched roofs, which had been the cause every year of conflagrations in thousands of villages; in increased purchases of clothes and jewelry, and in the crowds of noisy, cheery people that filled every bus and railway compartment on their way to weddings or on pilgrimages to Hindu shrines.

In spite of this steady progress, Indian poverty is in some ways worse today than it was fifty years ago. Four main causes may be isolated as accounting for the setback.

SETBACKS TO PROGRESS

¶ First, the Indian subcontinent has been passing through the change from a subsistence to a money economy and suffering all the accompanying crises. Until a few years ago, almost the whole of Indian agriculture was subsistence farming. The farmer with his few acres grew enough for himself and his family to live on and sold the scanty remainder in the local market or the nearest town; money transactions were few and not very important. Gradually all this changed; the Indian learned to grow crops for cash and to enter into world markets. East Bengal was found to be ideally suited to the growing of jute, and today produces the bulk of the world's jute crop. Much of the red soil in the south is excellent for the production of groundnuts. In Travancore hundreds of acres of fertile rice lands were transformed into coconut groves, since copra and coir for matting were found to be more profitable than rice. This did not seriously matter, as long as alternative sources of food supply were to be found.

But the increasing use of money was silently leading on to an unnoticed and pernicious social revolution. A money economy puts new power into the hands of the man who knows how to make money multiply itself. Debt is regarded in India more casually than in the West; the Indian peasant tends to borrow as much as he can. The "settlement," by means of which every scrap of land was registered by the government and the peasant's title to it made secure, as it had never been before, greatly increased his power of borrowing.

The fatal consequences were seen when the economic blizzard burst upon the world in 1929. Moneylenders and capitalists foreclosed mortgages, and the lands of the peasant were sold to meet his debts. This was entirely contrary to Indian tradition and resulted from the introduction of Western ideas of property and financial responsibility into a situation in which they were not at home. Hundreds of thousands of little men lost their lands and were transformed overnight from independent tillers of the soil into tenants-at-will on the lands that till recently they themselves had owned.

Before India had recovered from the financial storm, she was subjected to all the strains of the second world war. The war did not directly injure India, although the threat of Japanese invasion was serious for two long years. But capital enterprises languished. Worn-out locomotives on the railways could not be replaced. And, most serious of all, external sources of food supply were cut off.

Under stable administration, Lower Burma and the Delta of the Irrawaddy had been transformed into one gigantic rice field. Whenever food ran short in India, the government acquired stocks in Burma and made them available at reasonable prices. During the war, Burma suffered all the dislocations and injuries of Japanese occupation and a long, slow campaign of reconquest. As soon as peace returned, it decided to withdraw from the British Commonwealth and to set out on the path of total independence. The new state encountered chaos, disorder, and civil war, from which it has not yet recovered. Government control is still limited. What happens in Burma affects the whole future of Asia; it has long common frontiers with China, Indochina, Thailand, and Malaya. A Communist controlled Burma would menace the security of the whole of Southeast Asia. So far, Communist control has been only partial, but even so Burma in the postwar years grew hardly enough rice to feed itself and did not again become an exporting country until 1953. India, with a steady deficiency in food grains, had no readily available source of supply from which the deficit could be made good.

The third major factor is that the Department of Public Health has been doing a more successful job than the Department of Agriculture.[1] The population has begun to increase rapidly and to outgrow the food supply. Through the centuries incessant war, famine, and pestilence had kept the population almost stable. The British brought wars to an end; South India has had a longer period of unbroken peace than almost any other part of the world's surface. Famine was brought under control. A remarkably efficient health service dealt with the problems of plague and cholera and reduced both the frequency of epidemics and the severity of their incidence. Thereupon population began to increase by leaps and bounds; it has practically doubled itself in seventy years. The population of the Republic of India in 1951 was 361,821,624 and that of Pakistan 75,687,-000, a total of 437,508,624. Pressure of population on the soil is increasing. The standard of living, which was gradually rising, has begun catastrophically to fall.

The final blow has been the separation of India and Pakistan. Some idea of the difficulties introduced by partition can be realized by a single glance at the map. Pakistan consists of two areas, East and West, entirely different in character and traditions, separated from each other by a thousand miles of Indian territory. It is as though, in the period 1860-65, the southern states had

[1] It is interesting to note that the foundation of the Central Agricultural Institute at Pusa was made possible by a gift of $200,000 from an American, Mr. Phipps, to the then Viceroy of India, Lord Curzon.

been successful in separating themselves from the rest of the United States, and had then at the last moment been joined by Massachusetts and Rhode Island. Yet even this would not give a full idea of the difficulty of the situation, since the Atlantic sea lanes afford quick and easy communication between the North and the South. If we imagined an alliance between New England and California against the rest of the states, that might give a truer impression of the situation.

At the time of partition a great many people believed that Pakistan would never be able to exist as an independent state. Indeed, the difficulties she has had to face have been stupendous. The Muslims have in the past been great fighting men—but almost all the arsenals were in India, and such essential branches of modern armed forces as the air force, signals, and mechanical transport were almost wholly manned by Hindus and Christians. Almost all the bankers, and even the bank clerks, in Pakistan, were Hindus; with the mass exodus they left their work and returned to India. Almost all the insurance companies had their headquarters in India; many of them closed their Pakistani branches. East Pakistan grew the greater part of the world's jute crop, but had not a single jute mill for processing it; India had the jute mills with 57 per cent of the jute looms of the world, but hardly any jute to put into them.

And yet, in spite of all these drawbacks and absurdities, Pakistan has survived and held its own.

Those who predicted the speedy decline and dissolution of Pakistan had failed to notice that partition, for all its illogicalities, had given to Pakistan certain definite advantages, especially in the matter of food supply. For instance, most of the great dams and dikes already referred to are in Pakistan. In consequence, nearly three quarters of the sown area in West Pakistan has irrigational facilities, as compared with 22.5 per cent in the Indian provinces. In India an acre of rice yields 650 to 750 lbs., in Pakistan 850 to 900 lbs.; in India an acre of wheat yields 550 to 650 lbs., but in Pakistan 650 to 750 lbs. Cattle are fewer proportionately in Pakistan than in India, but the breeds are better, and the production of milk per head of milch cattle is greater. This means that the food situation in Pakistan, though far from satisfactory, is much better than in India and that it is to the needs of India that the sympathetic attention of the West must most urgently be directed. Failure of the rains in 1952 produced a serious, though probably temporary, crisis in Pakistan and made help from the United States urgently necessary. On May 25, 1953, President Eisenhower recommended that a million tons of wheat be made available to Pakistan.

In 1948 India imported 2.8 million tons of food stuffs, in 1949 she imported 3.7 millions. Government estimates for 1954 are optimistic, but it seems unlikely that any great reduction in imports will be practicable. Such figures do not mean much to the ordinary reader, and it may be helpful to break them down a little. A ton of foodstuffs will supply a good diet to three people for a year or to four and a half at the restricted level that is common throughout the whole of Asia. This means that, at the postwar rate of production, India was producing no food at all for twelve to fifteen million people, or that, if the whole population had to be fed from present supplies, the individual's ration would have to be reduced another 5 or 6 per cent below its present unsatisfactory level. And the population is increasing at the rate of nearly four million a year, requiring each year a further million tons of food to feed them. It is evident that India's major problem can be summed up in the simple words "Grow more food."

Grim as the problem is, it should not be assumed that it is insoluble. At present population presses heavily on soil, but as compared with many other countries, India, Pakistan, and Ceylon are not overpopulated. The density per square mile in 1951 appears to have been 296 in India, 210 in Pakistan [1] and 306 in Ceylon. This is heavy, when compared with about 50 in the United States, but favorable in contrast to Italy, with 397 to the square mile, or Great Britain, with 536. It is possible that, given the necessary improvements in methods and equipment, the Indian subcontinent could produce twice as much as it does today and support in comfort a considerably larger population. The question is whether the necessary progress will be made in time. All the three governments are aware that they are working against time and that it is hardly possible that everything necessary can be done without help from the world outside.

Mr. Gandhi took the view that India should turn its back on the perils of industrial civilization and go back to a simple peasant economy. Some of his faithful followers still hold firmly that he was right and view with anxiety and displeasure the increasing tendencies of government to fall in with Western ideas and policies. How much truth there was in Mr. Gandhi's ideas should be-

---

[1] But it is to be remembered that the density in West Pakistan is only 128 whereas in East Pakistan it is 772.

come clear later in the chapter, but for the moment even his own India is disinclined to follow him and regards Western technocracy not as an enemy to be feared but as the bringer of hope and new life.

FRESH ASSAULTS ON POVERTY

¶ If more food is to be grown in India, the first task is to increase the area of cultivable land. It must always be borne in mind that India, unlike Russia and the United States, is not a new, largely empty, and undeveloped country. The best of its lands have been occupied and cultivated for three thousand years; with the growth of population, all the easily cultivable lands have come under the plow or the spade. It is a case of creating a new world to supplement the old. The easiest way to do this is to carry on the great tradition of irrigation works, and to this governments have already set their hands. But the task is harder today than it was. "In India and Pakistan . . . practically all the low water flow of rivers is utilized for irrigation, except in the Ganges and the Brahmaputra. Future development must depend on storages of higher discharges and floods by reservoirs. The cost of irrigation by storage is usually higher than that by diversion." [1] Yet the higher cost is likely to be repaid by the benefits received; the experts calculate that so far only about 5 per cent of the water that flows down the Indian rivers has been made use of for the growth of crops, and that eventually at least ten times this amount should become available.

But irrigation is not the only benefit to be derived

[1] *Economic Survey of Asia and the Far East*, 1950 (United Nations, New York, 1951) p. 25.

from dams and dikes; they can be used also for the development of hydroelectric power. In this also a beginning was made long ago; the great hydroelectric station at the Pykara Falls in the Nilgiri Hills has supplied electric power to a wide area in South India. The extension of electric current was one of the few ways in which progress continued during the war. But India has available what must be an almost unlimited source of power. It has many of the highest mountains in the world and the highest rainfall (600 inches in a year at Cherrapunji in Assam). It is probable that less than 5 per cent of this potential is being used. If it can gradually be brought under control and made serviceable to man, the result will be a revolution in the economic situation of the subcontinent. The Damodar Valley project in West Bengal and Bihar has been deliberately planned as a multiple utility project, adopting some of the principles of the Tennessee Valley Authority.

It is a good thing to create new fields, but the fields must be fed and fertilized as well as made, and here we touch one of the most intractable of all the problems of India. In a land poor in mineral resources and almost treeless over large parts of its surface, it has long been the custom of the people to burn cow dung in their hearths. In consequence millions of tons of natural fertilizer, instead of being used to enrich the starving fields, have literally gone up in smoke.

To counteract this waste, governments are making strenuous efforts to encourage the planting of trees. On the annual *Vanamahotsavam*, everyone from the president down is expected to plant his tree. In that burning climate, trees need not merely to be planted but to be cared for tenderly for many months after, and for neglect of this care, the great majority of the trees die. Yet even so there is no doubt that this policy, persisted in for a generation, will greatly help the country, by the provision of timber, fuel, and additional supplies of manure.

Not content with this, the Indian government has called in science to supplement nature. On March 2, 1952, the Prime Minister pulled a lever at the fertilizer factory at Sindri in Bihar, and the first train of fertilizer steamed out of the yard. This factory, the largest of its kind in Asia and one of the largest in the world, was planned to deliver a thousand tons of ammonium sulphate a day. The factory was erected with American aid and was therefore described by Mr. Nehru as a "model of achievement born out of international fellowship in construction." [1]

It is often said that the remedy for Asian poverty is industrialization, and in the end this is no doubt true; the percentage of the population engaged solely in agriculture should be greatly reduced. But it is no use taking people off the land and setting them to industries if there is no food to sustain them and keep them alive while they work. It is often forgotten that in the West the agricultural revolution preceded the industrial and that the industrialization of America has been possible only because the number of people who can be fed by the labor of a single American farmer has been multiplied at least tenfold. It all comes back again to the question of growing more food.

If a nation is to be built anew, it must be built from

[1] *Embassy of India (Paris) Information Services*, March 5, 1952.

the base up, and that means starting with the peasant farmer as and where he is.

All the governments have in hand plans to reduce the indebtedness of the peasant and to restore him to the position of an independent proprietor by breaking up the great estates, with limited compensation to the owners, and distributing the land to those who will actually cultivate it.

The attention of the world has been drawn to this problem by the picturesque activities of one of the most faithful followers of Mr. Gandhi—Mr. Vinoba Bhave, a man of high education and culture, who has adopted a life of extreme simplicity and the traditional dress of the Indian holy man. Feeling that the plans of governments for the redistribution of land were going forward much too slowly, Mr. Bhave has traveled on foot through great tracts of India, pleading in every place with the landholders to surrender part of their lands freely for distribution to their poorer brethren. In many places his success has been sensational. His methods and the response to them are a reminder that the old India is still very much alive in the new. The holy man is endued with spiritual power, which he can use to the advantage or the detriment of those to whom he appeals. To give to a holy man adds merit to the account of the giver; by merit sins are taken away. It is possible that the landowners, who so generously responded to Mr. Bhave's persuasions, were swayed in part by motives of shrewd calculation as well as by generosity.[1]

[1] Mr. Bhave attained the unusual distinction of appearing on the cover of *Time* Magazine for May 11, 1953, which also contained a full though not altogether accurate account of his proceedings.

Distribution of land is good in that it tends to restore the great class of independent yeoman farmers. But of itself it will not solve the problem of food and may even accentuate it, since the small farmer cannot afford the mechanical aids and experimental methods that were used in the past by the more enlightened landowners. How to introduce such collective action as will make these necessary aids generally available, without infringing the new-found liberty of the cultivator, will be one of the most delicate problems to be faced by the governments of today and tomorrow.

No one, however, must imagine that prosperity is round the corner in South Asia, if only enough bulldozers and tractors can be introduced. Tropical soils demand to be treated with patience and respect. The model must be not the pioneer breaking down the virgin jungle of Brazil, but the Danes, who by patient tending and feeding of the soil over a century have turned the waste lands of Jutland into some of the finest dairy farming country in the world. There are plenty of warnings in the experiences of recent history for the man who would approach the Indian problem otherwise.

One enterprising farmer introduced heavier plows with a view to deeper plowing. He found that his bulls could not pull the new plows, so larger and stronger bulls had to be bought. The larger bulls ate more food and upset the delicate balance between food for man and food for beast. And when the deeper plowing had been carried out, the farmer found that in hot weather the plowed fields dried out to a level deeper than the roots of his crop could reach, and so they withered. The old shallow plow had left enough moisture near the surface to carry the crop through the burning days.

In addition to the difficulties provided by nature, there are others arising from the human material concerned.

First there is the conservatism of people long averse to change. A Swiss visitor to one of the projects of the World Health Organization twenty-five miles from Calcutta found that, although artesian wells had been constructed, many of the people still used for bathing and drinking the filthy pools from which mud for the walls of their houses had been dug. He saw that of 3,000 newly constructed latrines, the majority remained unused, since most of the people found it simpler to go into the fields as their ancestors had always done.[1]

Secondly (and it is hard for Americans to realize this), the ordinary Indian peasant does not want to get rich. He will work hard when it is necessary, but when he has done enough to keep himself and his family going, why should he do more? He is content with the few acres that his father left him. Bad seasons will come; they always have, and can be endured with the same stoicism that has made Indian society so stable for more than two thousand years. Part of the year he will be unemployed, but there are simple activities to make the days pass pleasantly. He will do minor jobs about the farm, gossip endlessly with neighbors under the great tree in the middle of the village, attend weddings, watch the performances of strolling players, and from time to time witness a really exciting lawsuit. He has the immense dignity of Abraham at the door of his tent, the

---

[1] *La Tribune de Genève*, May 1, 1952: "Où il faut une solide bicyclette pour combattre la maladie."

quiet assurance of a man who knows his established place in society and exactly fills it. Yet his calm is just beginning to be tinged with anxiety; he has an idea that the old days are coming to an end, that there will be no new lands for his sons to open up, and that the division of his fields after his death will not leave enough to keep the families of the new generation in any kind of comfort. It has taken a long time for the revolution to reach him, but reach him in the end it surely must.[1]

Thirdly, there is the inertia, in part due to malnutrition, which causes even people who have been shown better ways and helped to practice them to fall back into old habits, because too much effort is required to keep up with the new. It was this factor that largely frustrated the splendid work of Mr. F. L. Brayne, an ardent Christian and a distinguished member of the Indian Civil Service. While Mr. Brayne was commissioner of Gurgaon, one of the most backward districts in the Punjab, hundreds of manure pits were dug, silos constructed, better strains of seed and better breeds of cattle introduced. Within a few years the results were seen everywhere in enhanced prosperity in the villages. But when Mr. Brayne was transferred to another district, things fell back very much to what they had been before his coming. It was evident that too much had depended on the drive and initiative of one man and that the people had not become sufficiently convinced of the value of the new ways to continue in them after his influence had been withdrawn. As in the building up of

---

[1] This idyllic picture is true of millions of farmers in all the three countries, but obviously it is not true of the millions of tenants and landless laborers.

the Christian church, so in village uplift, it is necessary to work with unrelaxed effort over a period of thirty years, until a generation has grown up that has never known anything but the new life.

All these difficulties have to be borne in mind in estimating the value and the promise of the pilot projects for village renewal now being put into operation by some of the Indian governments. The best known of these, though it is only one of five similar projects, is the Etawah Project, launched in 1948 with American help in personnel though not in finance, by the government of Uttar Pradesh, formerly the United Provinces.

This scheme admirably meets the requirement of helping the villager by going to him where he is and planning in terms of life situations that he understands. Its director, Mr. Albert Mayer, has described the method as follows:

We must work with the people, not tell them. We must demonstrate by doing with our own hands in their own villages and fields—in short, "dirty hands" methods, not armchair methods. While a host of results may be achieved on the basis of initiative and organization by our workers . . . the work will not be permanent, there will not be a permanent awakening until the village develops its own leadership and initiative.[1]

In four years gratifying progress has been achieved. Output of the main crops has been increased by 30 to 40 per cent, and the Etawah area is not only meeting all its own needs but is beginning to supply others. Through the extension of green manuring the land is being

[1] Published in a supplement to the *Times of India*, August 15, 1952.

brought back into good heart. Spraying with simple chemicals is keeping pests under control. A new interest and spirit of cooperation in public works, such as roads, drainage, and primary schools, is beginning to manifest itself. Programs for adult literacy, village drama, and other cultural activities are being built up in some centers. The awakening is only in its beginnings, but it is a real awakening.

Missions and churches can only give thanks that governments are now taking up with enthusiasm a task in which the Christian forces have often given the lead. Unlike William Carey, some of the earliest missionaries contented themselves with preaching the gospel, in the belief that the moral transformation wrought by the gospel would in time solve economic and social problems. They were right in a sense, as all the evidence goes to show that economic help without moral transformation leads only to disappointing results. But gradually Christian leaders came to see that the gospel is directed toward the whole man and that the best technical assistance the West can provide can be set to the service of the gospel in helping those who are being morally transformed. Of the many enterprises sponsored by Christians in India, two may be singled out as examples.

Only a few miles from the southern tip of India, at Martandam in South Travancore, the Y. M. C. A. under the direction of Dr. Spencer Hatch built up its Rural Training Center. Here there was no great capital expenditure, no elaborate equipment; everything was kept as nearly as possible on the level of the village people themselves and the conditions under which they have to work. Villagers were shown ocularly the better results that they themselves could achieve by the adoption of more efficient methods in agriculture, gardening, the raising of poultry, and in other fields. The influence spread directly to the villages to a distance of thirty miles in all directions. Indirectly, through summer schools in which village pastors and teachers were introduced to the new ideas, it spread much more widely still.

More than a thousand miles to the north, outside Allahabad, close to what to Hindus is a most sacred spot, the confluence of the Jumna and Ganges, where at certain seasons literally millions of Hindu pilgrims gather to bathe in the sacred rivers, lay a large tract of derelict and apparently unusable land. The keen eye of Dr. Sam Higginbottom detected its possibilities. That desert is now the site of the great Agricultural Institute, at first an institution of the American Presbyterian Mission and now a union institute serving many missions and churches. Here agricultural education is carried out on the highest level, including courses leading to the university degree of Bachelor of Science in Agriculture. The institute trains able farmers, who will farm their own lands. It also produces the experts, who, in the service of the government Department of Agriculture or as teachers in other agricultural schools, will spread new ideas and better methods far afield through the country. The institute has just appointed its first Indian principal, Mr. Henry Azariah, the third son of the great Bishop Azariah of Dornakal.

A large grant from the Ford Foundation is making it possible for the institute to develop new projects that straitened finances had formerly rendered impossible of realization. And India is beginning to repay its debt to America, since hybrid strains of cattle reared at Allahabad are proving their worth in areas of the United States where agriculture is carried on under semi-tropical or almost tropical conditions.

Unfortunately, schemes for agricultural education and village uplift tend to be costly, especially at the start. Etawah is economically run, yet it costs something like $75,000 a year. This is a small sum in America but a large one in a poor country like India. Even if Etawah is multiplied a thousandfold, barely half the villages of India will have been touched; and the cost is prohibitive, unless very large sums, especially for capital expenditure, are made available from outside India.

TECHNICAL ASSISTANCE

¶ Here is one of the central problems of the present situation. The great development of India during the nineteenth century was made possible by the ready availability of Western, largely British, capital. Under an exceptionally able series of finance ministers, India was punctual in meeting all her financial obligations; until 1939 her credit stood high in world markets, and there was no difficulty in raising money for such creative works as railways and dams. Now all is changed. The generally unsettled condition of Southeast Asia, the danger of war between India and Pakistan, and wild talk in revolutionary days concerning the confiscation of foreign assets, have led the Western businessman to think that India is now a bad financial risk.

Probably the Indian subcontinent could in the end find the capital needed for its own development, but this would take a long time, and time is just what cannot be afforded; it is in delay that the greatest dangers lie. If India is to be saved, it can only be by the action of friendly governments, willing to make the necessary capital available on favorable terms and without making financial help an excuse for interference in the internal affairs of the three countries.

The first great step forward in international aid was the meeting of the foreign ministers of the British Commonwealth held at Colombo in January, 1950. "At this meeting the decision was taken to set up a Consultative Committee with the objects of surveying the needs of the area; and of providing the framework within which an international cooperative effort could be developed to assist the countries of South and Southeast Asia to raise the standard of living of their peoples." [1]

In September, 1950, the committee was ready with "The Colombo Plan for Cooperative Economic Development in South and Southeast Asia." Each government had been asked to prepare a six-year plan of urgent needs, relating mainly to "public investment for basic economic development on a large scale, in the fields of irrigation, power, communications, railways, roads, and other basic services, together with social development in health, education, housing, etc., which is an essential concomitant of economic progress." The plans drawn up by the governments did not cover all their needs,[2] but

[1] *The Colombo Plan* (a White Paper presented to Parliament, May, 1952), p. 4.
[2] The government of India was at the same time preparing its own far more comprehensive Five Year Plan for the development of all the resources of the country.

only such schemes as there was a reasonable hope of their completing within the six years that the plan was intended to cover. The total amount of capital needed was in the region of $5 billion, and of this it was reckoned that nearly half would have to come from outside the countries concerned.

The programs naturally vary a good deal from country to country. In India, the main emphasis is on irrigation, though with some attention to industrialization; Ceylon has included a scheme for the development of fisheries and one for the development of dry farming in an area of limited rainfall. The plans set forth by Pakistan are rather more varied, and include:

Construction of commercial dry dock, Karachi
Purchase of fifteen ocean going steamers
Purchase of three Convair aircraft
A telephone factory
Cement, two factories
Jute mills, four
Antimony refining plant
Purchase of equipment for animal husbandry

It may be interesting to look at these plans from the other end and to consider the contribution of one dominion to the welfare of others. New Zealand is the smallest of the dominions, with a population considerably less than that of the state of Connecticut. It has agreed to provide roughly 3 million dollars a year for the first three years of the Colombo Plan.

At the same time, New Zealand is taking part in the technical assistance scheme set up under the Colombo Plan. During 1953, fifty students from India, Pakistan, and Ceylon were in New Zealand, taking courses in graduate nursing and dental nursing, diseases of women and maternal and child care, aspects of animal husbandry, engineering, school organization, housing, social services and public administration, factory and sanitary inspection, factory management, pharmacology, chemical analysis of minerals, and statistical organization.[1] When it is remembered that New Zealand is the smallest of the dominions and that these students represent only three of the Southeast Asian countries, the total impact and potentialities of the Colombo Plan can well be imagined.

The most satisfactory feature of all is the spirit of mutual respect and helpfulness in which the plans are being carried through. In March, 1952, at the fourth meeting of the Consultative Committee held at Karachi (at which Burma and Nepal were represented for the first time), the Pakistani minister for economic affairs, Mr. Fazlur Rahman, who presided, said in his final speech that there was no feeling of superiority attached to the act of giving or inferiority tainting the act of receiving, but that the members of the plan were working as members of a family imbued with the idea of helping one another.

It is against this background of common sense, practical and realistic long term planning, well established fellowship, and mutual respect, that the question of American help to India and the other countries has to be considered.

It is deeply disturbing to Americans to discover that, in spite of their generous giving and high ideals, they

[1] *The Round Table,* September, 1952, p. 387.

are regarded with suspicion in many countries, as the purveyors of an economic imperialism even more dangerous than the old political imperialism that has already passed away. Many have felt that America is interested only in America, that other countries are considered only as outer bastions in the American scheme of defense, and that their peoples and their civilizations are regarded as expendable, if America itself should be seriously threatened.

It is tragic that this should be so, but such psychological considerations are sometimes more important even than the economic and social factors with which this chapter is concerned. American senators and representatives, who dragged out the long and weary debates on the question of making available two million tons of wheat to India, at a time when people were literally dying in the streets, probably did not realize that their least considered words were being reproduced by the press in India and were making the worst possible impression on the minds of the people.

One single new factor made possible the beginning of an improvement in Indian-American relations—the character and personality of Mr. Chester Bowles, former American ambassador at Delhi. The sympathy and genuine kindliness of the ambassador, what an observer in India has called "his engaging enthusiasm for this country," his diligence and persistence in advocating his views, did wonders in convincing India that there are Americans who are really interested in India for her own sake and whose help can be accepted without either the sacrifice of national pride or hidden perils to independence.

At the third meeting of the Colombo Plan Committee representatives of the United States were present. From that time on American help has been growing in strength and usefulness. The eventual grant of a loan of $190 million to India for the purchase of wheat was timely aid. Other loans have been granted, and the exchange scheme of experts and students is working well. In 1952 more than three hundred Indian students under the U. S. Educational Foundation in India were undergoing training in the United States.

A considerable step forward was taken with the signing by Mr. Bowles and Mr. Nehru, on January 5, 1952, of the Indo-U.S. Technical Cooperation Agreement. "Recognizing that individual liberty, free institutions, and independence on the one hand, and sound economic conditions and stable international economic relationships on the other hand, are mutually interdependent," the two governments agreed to put into execution a reconstruction scheme that is planned to affect 17,500 villages, with a population of twelve million people. The plan is for fifty-five units of about three hundred villages each, mostly located near to the irrigation or river valley projects that are already planned or in execution. The aim is the increase of production from already cultivated land, the extension of cultivable areas, the raising of the standard of living of the people, and the establishment of a stable balance between the urban and rural communities.

Can all this be done? Here as elsewhere, the moral and spiritual factors are as important as the natural and the economic.

These plans will succeed only along the lines of what

Mr. Mayer calls "dirty-hand methods." The nations of Southeast Asia would rather go poor and hungry than submit to the patronage of richer and more fortunate peoples. They will welcome the generous service of those who like them for themselves, who are willing to work on their level, side by side with them, and to manifest the spirit of a genuine and simple equality.

The future depends on the development of a new spirit of hope and enterprise in the Asian peoples themselves. No permanent advance can be made simply by doing things for people from outside; the outside help is valuable only if it sets up in the minds and lives of the people themselves a ferment that will continue long after external aid has been withdrawn. All these projects can be wrecked on the old rock of corruption; their success will depend on an army of incorruptible, efficient, and self-sacrificing administrators. Can such be found in sufficient numbers? In the great days of Mr. Gandhi, the Congress Party did succeed in infusing a high and noble spirit into its workers, but since independence there has been all too much evidence of the failure of this spirit among the rank and file. What are the spiritual resources from which it can be renewed and kept in being?

This is a subject on which the Christian churches may well have something to say.

3

The Church in Southern Asia

THREE CHRISTIAN GROUPS

No one knows how many Christians there are in India, Pakistan, and Ceylon. The last census to give reasonably reliable religious statistics was that of 1931; at that time there were just under six million Christians in what we were then still able to call India. It appeared that, in the ten years 1921-31, the Christian community had grown by 32 per cent and the non-Roman churches 45 per cent. The religious statistics in the 1941 census were hopelessly inaccurate; those from the census of 1951, while less inaccurate than those of 1941, still erred by gravely understating the number of Christians in India. The editors of the *Directory of Churches and Missions in India and Pakistan, 1951*, working along various lines of computation, have concluded that the rate of Christian advance has slowed down a little, but that it is fairly safe to reckon that by 1941 there were eight million Christians and by 1951 ten millions in the two countries. To these must be added about 700,000 in Ceylon. Thus at the time of publication of this book we may reckon with a growing Christian fellowship in the three countries of between eleven and twelve million, the total population now being about 445 million, more than two and a half times that of the United States. To put it in another way, about one person in every thirty-eight in the three countries is a Christian at least in name. Not less than 97 per cent of the population is still non-Christian.

Figures are useful, as giving a rough indication of the situation, but they need much interpretation if we are to have any real idea of the state of the churches in the three countries in 1954. One of the crimes of mission boards is that they frequently publish maps of the areas entrusted to them showing only the work for which they are responsible and giving no hint that other churches and missions are at work in the same areas. This makes it almost impossible for supporters of missions to become aware of the total situation, in the light of which the efforts of their own church have to be understood. We must start by trying to give, as fairly as possible, an outline of the total impact of the Christian message on the Indian subcontinent.

The Christian community in India, Pakistan, and Ceylon falls into three main divisions.

First there is the very ancient church of Malabar, mainly in Travancore and Cochin in the southwest, all the members of which are convinced that their church was founded by the Apostle Thomas in person. Whether this be so or not, it is certain that Christian churches have existed in that area and have had a continuous history since the fourth century A.D. at latest. This church, because of its age-long connection with Mesopotamia, is generally called the Syrian Church; although it is probable that the earliest Christians in India were Syrian merchants, the name is misleading, since the church has been for centuries purely Indian. Travancore is quite unlike any other part of India. Nearly one third of the population is Christian; here alone in India one sometimes has the feeling of being in a Christian country.

Unhappily, the ancient church has become very much divided. In 1599 it was completely absorbed by the Roman Catholic Church, and though fifty-four years later a large section broke away again into independence, half the Syrians are still Romo-Syrians. The largest section of the independent Syrians is known as the Malankara Church and numbers about half a million people. This group has become bitterly divided within itself; one section wished to develop a more constitutional form of government and to limit the authority over it of the patriarch of Antioch, who lives in Homs in Syria; the other section was prepared to maintain the rights of the patriarch unimpaired. The disputes have led to long litigation in the secular courts as to the ownership of the property of the church; recently the Supreme Court of Travancore decided in favor of the patriarch's party and handed over almost all the property to what is actually the smaller of the two sections. The case has now gone up on appeal to the Supreme Court of India. Many faithful Christians, particularly in the younger generation, have looked on with disgust at these endless legal proceedings before non-Christian judges, which have brought discredit on the Christian name and have grievously depleted the finances of the church. Various efforts have been made to reconcile the contending factions, but so far all in vain.

The Mar Thoma Syrian Church, with about 250,000 adherents, came into separate existence about sixty years ago, as a result of a reforming movement within the ancient church, which owed much to the influence of the Anglican missions. This church, which represents the unusual combination of a simple biblical faith with the elaborate traditions of Eastern worship, has always been marked by intense evangelistic activity.

For centuries, these ancient churches had been hidden behind the mountains in Travancore. Now the situation is rapidly changing. This part of India has the highest percentage of educated persons in the country; the percentage of literacy is especially high among Christians. Educated Syrian Christians in large numbers have gone to other parts of India in search of work, and there is hardly a city in India in which a group of Syrians will not be found, playing an important part in the affairs both of church and state. The late Sarah Chakko, principal of Isabella Thoburn College for Women, Lucknow, and one of the presidents of the World Council of Churches, was an Orthodox Syrian Christian of Malabar. Inevitably this extension of interests is bringing to the church a new sense of responsibility in relation to India as a whole. For centuries the Syrians had done little or nothing for the spread of the gospel, even among the Hindus at their doors. Now they are beginning to feel that God had a special purpose in preserving them through all the centuries of their isolation. As a church distinctively Indian and free from the foreign aspect that attaches to all the churches more recently founded by missions from the West, they can fulfill a special task in independent India.

The second great section of Indian Christianity is the Roman Catholic Church. When Vasco da Gama rounded the Cape of Good Hope and cast anchor off Calicut in 1498, there were priests aboard his ships. From that time on, the Roman Catholic Church has had extensive work in India, its earliest center being Goa, which is still the capital of Portuguese India. The first conspicuous success was the conversion in 1534 of the entire Fisher caste of the southeast coast. This first movement was undoubtedly superficial and influenced more by political than by religious motives; but eight years later the new Christians were organized by the great Francis Xavier, and their descendants have remained faithful to their church through more than four centuries. At the present time, almost exactly half the Christians in India are Roman Catholics.

In recent years a remarkable change has come over the Roman Church in India. One or two Indian priests were made bishops in the seventeenth and eighteenth centuries. Then the experiment was given up, and thirty years ago, except for some Indian bishops of the Romo-Syrian group, all the Roman Catholic bishops in India were Europeans. Pope Pius XI, realizing the great dangers that might befall a church so wholly dependent on European direction, personally took the initiative in changing this situation. He insisted that an Indian episcopate must be created as quickly as possible, in order that the Indian church might have within itself the completeness of Christian life as that is understood in the Roman Church. The first Indian diocesan bishop of the Latin rite was appropriately a descendant of the early converts of 1534, Mgr. Tiburtius Roche, who became bishop of

Tuticorin, a port town in the far south, in 1923. From that time on, progress has been extremely rapid. Hardly a year has passed without the creation of a new bishopric, the first bishop in most cases being an Indian. Now the process is being carried a step further, and Indians are being appointed to such great historic sees as Bombay and Colombo. In 1952 there were twenty-three Indian Roman Catholic bishops. The year 1953 saw the creation of the first Indian cardinal.

This change is giving to the Roman Catholic Church a more distinctively Indian character than it has ever had before. For centuries all Indian priests have been trained exactly as priests are trained in Italy or in America. It has been their business to learn Latin, to study St. Thomas Aquinas and the fathers, and to follow exactly the traditions of the West. They have had little time or impulse to penetrate deeply into the mind and thought of India or to find an Indian expression for the Christian faith. Now Indian Roman Catholics are beginning to recognize that their church must become really at home in India. They must master the ancient classics; they must be alert to the new currents of thought that are sweeping across the country; without altering the essential content of the faith, they must find new ways of appealing to the heart and mind of modern India.

Traditionally, the Roman Catholic Church had not done much for the education of its people, other than candidates for the priesthood, with the result that, of the Christians who have played outstanding parts in the life of India, comparatively few have been Roman Catholics. This situation began to change toward the end of the nineteenth century when the Jesuits, moved perhaps by the success of the Protestant Christian colleges, began to set up their own colleges in the great centers of their faith. The figures for 1951 show 42 Roman Catholic colleges of university status, educating more than 22,000 students, of whom 3,600 are girls; of the student body, about a quarter are Roman Catholics, 10 per cent are Christians of other churches, and just under two thirds are non-Christians. From these 5,000 Roman Catholic students will be drawn the elite of the Indian Roman Catholic Church of the future, and many among them will find their way to positions of influence in government, in the learned professions, and in every part of the life of the three countries.[1]

When compared with the orderly and disciplined progress of Roman Catholic work, the missions of the non-Roman churches present a sadly casual and disordered appearance. The work is carried on by more than a hundred missionary societies, apart from special enterprises such as the great union colleges; these are drawn from almost every country in the Protestant world and represent all the main denominations, as well as many of the small ones. The early scandals of competition, overlapping, and "sheep stealing" have to a large extent been eliminated by successive comity agreements, under which one mission does not enter fields

[1] It should be explained that the majority of the Indian universities are of the affiliating type; thus colleges attached to Madras University are found all over Madras State, the students all taking the examinations set by the university in Madras and receiving their degrees from it. There is no Christian degree-giving university in India. Serampore College, under its Danish charter, gives degrees in divinity only.

where others are already at work, but even now there is a great deal of wasteful overlapping and duplication of work. It is still difficult to secure cooperative action even on the part of missions in the same territory. Strategic planning for the spread of the gospel throughout the whole of the three countries has not yet been developed, and, as long as Protestant indiscipline (independence, some would prefer to call it) remains as strong as it is, such planning is likely to remain an unrealized vision.

Non-Roman missions are to be found in almost every part of India. But a map shaded to indicate the strength of the Christian occupation would reveal remarkable unevenness, both in the distribution of the forces of the Protestants and in the success accorded to their efforts.

Christians are far more numerous in the south than in the north, and in general it may be said that the further north one goes, the fewer the Christians are likely to be. Why this is so, it is difficult to say; it just happened that till quite recently all the great movements toward the Christian faith took place in the south. As we have seen, the ancient Syrian Church existed only in the far southwest. The first great Roman Catholic movement was in the far southeast. Just at the end of the eighteenth century, a remarkable stirring in the Tinnevelly District, close to the southern tip of India, brought thousands of people into the Anglican Church and laid the foundations for what is now the Tinnevelly Diocese of the Church of South India. From the end of the nineteenth century onward, a great mass movement in the Telugu country north of Madras brought a million people into the Protestant churches. Great movements have taken place also in Uttar Pradesh and in the Punjab, the latter having increased the number of Christians in the Punjab more than tenfold in the present century. But it still remains true that on the whole the Christian movement is far weaker in the north than in the south.

NOT MANY NOBLE

¶ Christianity is in the main a religion of the simple and the poor, and has hardly touched the adherents of the three great classical religions of the subcontinent. Ceylon is mainly Buddhist, India mainly Hindu, and Pakistan mainly Muslim. Each of these three great religions is a compact social system as well as a religion, controlling and directing the lives of its adherents at every point and in every way. Converts have been won from them all, and these converts and their descendants have provided most of the leadership in the South Asian churches. But their numbers have always been small. The gospel has as yet hardly shaken these great fortresses, and the nineteenth century expectation that, in the face of Christian truth, these ancient systems would crumble away, has not as yet even begun to be fulfilled. No one church can claim to have been more successful than any other in the approach to the Brahman, the Muslim, and the Buddhist. Every type of Christian faith has been engaged in the work of preaching the gospel; every method has been tried, from the learned approach of the scholar missionary who could speak Sanskrit as well as the Hindu religious scholar to the simple unsophisticated testimony of the Salvation Army. Each has won some converts; none has been able on any large scale to break through the firm, consistent resistance of the Eastern faiths.

If the missions have failed to win the higher castes and the educated classes, it has not been for want of trying. It is often stated that the missionaries, finding such work difficult, hardly attempted it, and directed their efforts to the poor and the outcaste. This is almost exactly the opposite of the truth. Almost every mission started by approaching the higher castes, in the hope that once converted they would set themselves to the task of winning their poorer brethren. The first convert of Carey and his friends at Serampore was Krishna Pal, the Brahman. Although India is a land of villages, the majority of Protestant missionaries have always been found in the towns, and an immense amount of effort has been expended on educational work, from which the higher castes have profited more than others. When movements started among the poor and underprivileged, they were rarely the result of a direct approach, and they were by no means always welcome to the missionaries and Indian leaders who had to deal with them. If the existing Indian church is largely the result of mass movements among the outcastes, that must be attributed, not to planning, but only to what came in time to be recognized as an irresistible movement of the Spirit of God.

It is not surprising that many missionaries did not at first think of the approach to the outcastes as a hopeful method of winning India for Christ. Under the influence of the gospel the depressed and underprivileged have proved that they are not inferior in native capacity to their richer neighbors and that, given opportunity, they can develop every Christian virtue and every human talent. But even now it is only the eye of faith that can discern these possibilities. For centuries these people have been denied every human privilege, cut off from every social or economic advantage, condemned to live in grinding poverty, perpetually on the border line of starvation. Worst of all, their plight was rendered unalterable through its connection with religion.

They have been held in their shameful plight by all the holy principles of religion and the most sacred laws of society. Their masters have charged them in the name of God and of humanity to remain in their abasement and taught them that it was a sin to attempt deliverance from their degradation, that by all they held sacred they were bound by their chains forged by the supreme law of *Karma*.[1]

The sixty million untouchables are scattered over almost the whole of the subcontinent, living sometimes in separate villages, sometimes on the fringe of the villages of the higher castes. They have their place in the Hindu scheme, since it is theirs to perform the essential tasks of the barber, the washerman, and the scavenger. In return they receive a minimum recognition of rights and support. And just because they live so close to their masters and overlords, they have potentially a remarkable power for Christian witness. If conversion to Chris-

[1] *The Children of Hari*, by Stephen Fuchs. Quoted by L. W. Bryce in the *National Christian Council Review*, Nov. 1951, p. 499. Used by permission.

Karma is the law of retribution, the belief that all troubles and misfortunes in this life are the fruit of sins committed in a previous existence. We are here writing of the nineteenth and early twentieth centuries; the great work of Mr. Gandhi on behalf of the untouchables has helped to change the situation, and in the Indian constitution "untouchability" has been abolished. However, such a change in principle does not penetrate quickly to the unchanging life of an Indian village, and the latest reports indicate that in practice the condition of the untouchables remains very much what it was before.

tianity means a real change in their moral standards and behavior, this immediately becomes evident to their masters. More of the higher castes have been brought to Christian faith by the witness of changed lives than through the direct testimony of the missionary.

The untouchables, however, are not the only group whose response to the preaching of the gospel has made this work among them conspicuously successful. India is a land of innumerable peoples and languages. With the spread of wave after wave of invasion from the north and west, there has always been a tendency for the weaker and less developed peoples to be driven back into the jungles and the hills. There they still live in their millions. Some, like the Gonds, Bhils, and Santals, are considerable peoples, with independent traditions and languages of their own and a sense of dignity that has kept them almost completely free from the servility into which the untouchables have been ground down. Others are small tribes, broken fragments of greater peoples, crushed in war and exiled from the more fertile lands that their fathers once owned.

Most of these tribes and peoples lead a life that by Western standards is simple and primitive, but this is by no means to say that they are savages. All are alike in having remained to a large extent untouched by the traditions of the three great classical religions. They belong to the animistic level, with its belief in the spirits of wood and spring and mountain, many of them malevolent, some more kindly, and with sometimes in the background the sense of one great God to whom in some way both men and spirits are subject. Throughout history, Hinduism has been spreading among these peoples, and some have been gradually assimilated into the all embracing Hindu system of caste. In other cases the gospel got there first and touched these peoples before other influences began to change their traditions and their old simple way of living.

As with the untouchables, in most cases missionaries did not deliberately seek out these remote peoples, but were brought into touch with them almost by chance. A typical case is that of the tribal peoples of Bihar, the Mundas, the Oraons, and the Hos. The German missionaries of the Gossner Mission started work among the Hindu caste people of the great northern plain and labored for many years almost without success. About the middle of the nineteenth century, they began to advance into the highlands, where they learned the tribal languages and started preaching to the simple people in their own tongue. Almost immediately the tribesmen began to respond. In less than a century great churches, numbering hundreds of thousands of members, divided between the Lutherans, the Anglicans, and the Roman Catholics, have come into being. The Gossner Evangelical Lutheran Church declared itself autonomous on July 10, 1919, and, though it still welcomes the help of missionaries from the West, it is a wholly independent and self-governing Indian Church.[1]

The situation in Assam, the northeast corner of India, is very similar. In the plains work had been carried on for a century with the greatest faithfulness but with small results. But when American Baptist missionaries entered the Sadiya area, Welsh Presbyterian missionaries

[1] *World Christian Handbook* (1952) gives the number of its adherents as 186,447.

penetrated into the Khasi hills, and the American and English Baptists into the Lushai, Garo, and Naga hills and other mountain tracts on the very frontier of Burma, everything was changed. Hundreds of thousands of converts have been won among these mountain peoples, and these new Christians themselves have set out to win others. Here is a vivid picture from the pen of a visitor, Bishop George Sinker of Nagpur, of the life and vigor of these new Christian groups:

There can be few things more thrilling and more satisfying than to see the Lord Jesus Christ capture whole tribes and transform not only individual lives, but the whole tribal way of life. It was our wonderful experience to meet huge congregations of head-hunters turned into soul winners. . . . There is no indication that the tribes are dying out; on the contrary, they are a virile and growing community and as Christians are likely to have an important effect on Indian history. Many of these tribes are more than half Christian already; almost all are affected in a greater or less degree. . . . The church is growing rapidly, and this growth is often only indirectly the work of the foreign missionary. One of the most outstanding facts about this magnificent church is that it is self-propagating. Within a few miles of Impur lies a completely unadministered area on the borders of India and Burma. No foreigner is allowed into this area, and head-hunting still continues unchecked. But the Christian tribesmen on each side of the border are infiltrating where no missionary can go and establishing Christian congregations in village after village in this wild area. . . . Here in the Assamese Hills the Christian church worships, witnesses, gives, and plans its own extension, without waiting for a lead from the missionary. . . . Is this the key to the evangelization of northern India? Young men and women of these tribes are coming down to the Indian universities in ever increasing numbers. If therefore these tribes do in any way constitute a strategic base for Christian advance, then their Christian life and worship must be built up and consolidated around the complete word of God in their own languages as soon as possible.[1]

All that the good bishop has written is true, but this wonderful record must not conceal from us the labors and struggles that have had to be passed through before the churches could reach the happy condition that he has described. The comparative failure of missionary work among the well-to-do and its success among the disinherited and the remote presented the Indian church with three gigantic problems. These millions of converts were almost all animists, their minds filled with superstitious fears. How, even among the Christians, could the old ancestral fears and the practices to which they gave rise be finally cast out and the people that sat in darkness brought into the full light of Christ? Almost all these people were exceedingly poor. How could the churches founded among them ever become self-supporting? They were almost wholly illiterate. Can an uneducated church survive, against the overwhelming pressure of the non-Christian world around it?

THE LIVING WORD IN LIVING LANGUAGES

¶ Unlike the Roman Catholics, Protestant missionaries from the beginning believed that many problems could be solved by giving the people the Word of God in their own languages as soon as possible. But it is no use giving people the Bible unless they can read it. From the very start of the non-Roman missionary enterprise

[1] *Nagpur Diocesan Magazine*, July, 1952, pp. 57-58. Used by permission.

in India, church and school have been inseparable components of the enterprise. Some years ago, in the Lutheran mission compound at Tranquebar, where the first Protestant missionaries settled in 1706 and where the first translation of the New Testament into any Indian language was made and printed, twenty-one coats of whitewash were stripped off an ancient building, and there over the door were revealed in eighteenth century lettering the words *Dharmappallikkudam* (charity school). In Tranquebar the school even antedates the church.

Missions had been carrying on schools long before the government took a hand in the game. But a great new opportunity was offered to the missionaries when in the middle of the nineteenth century British educational policy in India was formulated. The government did not attempt itself to build up a national system of education. True to its perhaps exaggerated belief in free enterprise, it preferred to leave most of the work to private individuals or bodies but was willing to assist them. It was laid down that financial aid would be given to any school, by whatever agency it might be conducted, that would accept inspection by government inspectors and conform to syllabuses of instruction laid down by the Department of Public Instruction. Few restrictions, if any, were placed in the way of religious instruction in the schools.

Almost all missions in India, in spite of some natural hesitation, especially on the part of the Free Church missions, at allying themselves with so dangerous a power as the government, decided to grasp this new opportunity. Within a few years, mission schools with government aid were numbered by thousands. **Over** large areas every single school was a mission **school,** in which children of all religions, and often of **many** different castes, sat together and studied the Bible **to-** gether. Often the building was no more than a mud hut with thatched roof, equipment was primitive in the extreme, and teaching methods archaic. But in many areas the hero of the growth of the Indian church is the village teacher, helped by his wife. Often he is charged with almost all the duties of an ordained minister in addition to the work of the school. He is sometimes lazy or incompetent, generally marvelously faithful and devoted, always on the spot, and always representing to the most simple and backward community something of the light of Christ and the preciousness of knowledge.

The Protestant churches of South Asia have been based on the Bible, the little group of worshiping believers, and the village school. But on that foundation an immense superstructure of educational, medical, and social service has gradually been built up. To those who ask, "Why do not the churches or the missions do this or that?" the answer in almost every case is that the churches and missions, hampered as they are and always have been by lack of funds and personnel, are already doing that very thing.

Here are a few facts to justify this statement and to indicate the range and variety of contemporary Christian enterprise. The non-Roman churches in India and Pakistan today maintain 67 agricultural settlements or farm colonies. They possess 42 printing presses. They support 92 industrial or trade schools for boys and girls. They are responsible for 277 hospitals, to a large number of which institutions for the training of nurses are attached, a much larger number of dispensaries, 70 homes or special hospitals for lepers, twelve tuberculosis sanatoria, and nine schools for the deaf or blind. Some of these institutions are small; many of them are less efficient than those responsible for them could wish. But this bare list of figures may serve to indicate that the church is trying to touch the life of India at every point and to fit Christians to serve their country in every possible capacity.

But our immediate concern is with education in the narrower sense of the term, and here, too, the figures of the educational pyramid are impressive. Above the village schools come the middle schools, up to the eighth year of education; of these the churches maintain many hundreds. Above the middle school comes the high school, and at this level the churches have 383 schools for boys and girls in India and Pakistan, not including Ceylon. One hundred and nine teachers' training institutions prepare the teachers for work in these various schools. And finally we reach the Christian college affiliated with an Indian university. The non-Roman churches are responsible for 43 such colleges, to be found in every province and major area of the subcontinent. The figures published in 1951, the latest available to me, show that 22,278 students were being educated in these colleges, of that number 3,427 being women students and 4,040 Christian students. Of a total staff of 1,244, there were 596 Christians, and among these the Indian Christians outnumbered their missionary colleagues by more than three to one. The steady increase in recent years in the proportion of women students to men and of Christian to non-Christian students and teachers has been impressive.

The result of this immense educational effort, carried on for more than two centuries but with greatly increased impetus in the last fifty years, has been in almost every area to raise the average standard of education among Christians high above that of the surrounding non-Christian population. There is no ground, however, for complacency. The rapid membership increase in mass movement areas has gone far beyond the capacity of the church to deal with it, and illiteracy in the church remains one of the greatest dangers to the Christian movement in India.[1]

Many educated Christians have found their vocation in whole time service to the church. Others have attained the highest distinction in other walks of life. The first Indian governor of Bombay was Raja Sir Maharaj Singh, a descendant of the princely house of the state of Kapurthala and a licensed lay reader of the Anglican church in India. In 1951, Dr. H. C. Mukerjee, formerly a professor at the University of Calcutta and a member of a Baptist church, became governor of West Bengal, a state with a population of almost twenty-five million people. In the first all-India cabinet of independent India, the minister of health is an Indian Christian woman, the Rajkumari Amrit Kaur, a sister of Sir Maharaj Singh. One of the ministers in the first independent government of Madras was Mr. Daniel Thomas, a distinguished lawyer, who owned a library of nearly

[1] The great work of Dr. Laubach in promoting literacy is well known in America, and consideration of space has made it impossible to deal with it in detail here.

four thousands books in English, the great majority of which he had read.

These outstanding members lend distinction to the church. It is, however, even more important that education has brought into being a great Christian middle class of doctors, lawyers, civil servants, teachers, and other professional men and women. This middle class is always one of the most stable elements in society. Also the middle class, unlike the cultivator of the soil who tends to be tied to his father's lands, is mobile, and goes far and wide in search of work. As a result of this migratory tendency of the educated Christian, there is in the subcontinent scarcely a township of five thousand inhabitants or over that has not its little Christian group —perhaps a police officer, a nurse in the government hospital (till recently Christian girls have had almost a monopoly of the nursing profession), a ticket agent at the depot, or a sanitary inspector. These groups, living in places where no missionary has ever penetrated and sometimes many miles from the nearest ordained minister, are not always as alive or filled with evangelistic zeal as they should be, but there they are, a sign of Christian penetration, and an unobserved and often disregarded factor in the spread of the gospel throughout the country.

A VILLAGE CHURCH

¶ But in the main the Christian church in India and Pakistan (much less so in Ceylon) is a village church. Three quarters of the population lives in villages, and the Christians are fairly typical of the population as a whole. It is reckoned that there are Christian groups worshiping regularly in nearly 30,000 of the 750,000 villages of the subcontinent. The majority of these groups consist of between 150 and 250 people, living in the midst of a large majority of non-Christian neighbors. There are some wholly Christian villages, especially in the areas where social pressure has been such as to make it necessary for Christians to leave their homes and to found new communities without roots in the past. Everywhere the center of life is the church, which may be the only building of brick or stone in the village; and just because life is simpler and often duller than in the towns, the church with its recurring festivals and ceremonies means more to the people living about it than is the case in the more sophisticated West.

Complaints are often made of the foreignness of the church in India. They are rarely made by those who have dwelt long in the villages and have come to feel their atmosphere. Here the church is not foreign; it is closely, sometimes too closely, integrated with the life of the community. It is from this closeness of contact that many of the tensions and problems of the growing Indian church derive.

India is in ferment, and change is extremely rapid. Yet little of this change has as yet reached the village, which tends to go on very much in ancestral ways. The framework of village life is the caste system, the ancient organization of society, partly on the basis of crafts and vocations, partly on the basis of mutual obligation and services, which has given wonderful stability to Indian society for two thousand years and has also been a most potent factor in slowing down or preventing change.

The members of the caste feel themselves to belong to one another as brothers and sisters, and even though they may quarrel among themselves, they will display intense loyalty in standing by one another against the outside world. They share a host of common customs in dress, in idiom of speech, and in the ritual connected with birth, puberty, marriage, and death, as well as a common occupation. Common ethical standards are maintained by the elders of the caste, and the ordinary man fears a *panchayat* [1] of his own caste (which can finally outcaste him) more than a government official who may merely send him to prison. . . . Of course, like the village community, the caste system has been under heavy and damaging attack. . . . Yet the ancient system is still enormously strong.[2]

Almost every Indian Christian in the villages knows to what caste he belongs and feels a loyalty to it. He may feel greater kinship with Hindu members of the same caste than with Christians outside his caste. This is typical of the tensions within which the Indian Christian must live and of the direct and creative challenge that the gospel presents to every non-Christian system.

The Christian is immediately aware of his special responsibility in relation to the Christian group in his village. But he cannot detach himself from the general life of the village, on which in so many ways he is dependent, though his relationship to the non-Christian part of the community may be severely strained in times of persecution or hostility. He feels a kinship with all the members of his own caste wherever they may be; yet

[1] The group usually composed of five elders, which exercises local authority in the village or community.

[2] *That All May Be One,* by J. E. Lesslie Newbigin, pp. 48-49. A Haddam House Book, New York, Association Press, 1952. Used by permission.

he is well aware that the church transcends caste and includes members of many castes, to whom he cannot remain indifferent and whom he cannot treat as though they had nothing to do with him. Patriotism is a growing force in India, but even the simplest Christian knows that he belongs to a world wide community, which denies the absoluteness of any local or geographical loyalty and which may have become a visible reality to him in a missionary whom he has come to know and love as a friend. Finally there is the tension between the traditional and the personal. The corporate life of an Indian village, with its endless caste rules and customs, weighs heavily on personal life and gives little scope for individual decision or responsibility. The Christian knows that he is responsible for his actions in the sight of God, and that, if at any point old custom and the demands of God are at variance with each other, it is the demands of God that must be obeyed.

It is because of these tensions, and particularly of the last, that Bishop Newbigin is justified in writing:

> We are still at the dawn of history here in these villages. A tremendous ferment is at work, and it is impossible to predict the future. . . . Something like a truly indigenous Christian culture is to be found here, though it is not what is often sought for by that name. The gospel is here present and operative at what looks like a vital growing point in human history.[1]

This striking passage indicates the creative task that the small churches in India, Pakistan, and Ceylon are called to carry out in the midst of the whirlwind of change and new development that has suddenly come

---

[1] *Ibid.*, p. 50. Used by permission.

upon their countries. How far are the spiritual resources of these churches adequate to the task that they have to undertake today?

THE CALL TO RENEWAL

¶ The existence of the younger churches is an outstanding miracle. When we consider the difficulty of winning even a single convert, the many areas in which missionaries have labored faithfully over a whole generation without seeing even the beginnings of an indigenous church, the ceaseless opposition and hostility of which Christians have been the victims, the penetrating, weakening influence of the non-Christian environment, the perennial shortage in missionary personnel and funds, it is astonishing that there should be eleven or twelve million Christians in the three countries today.

It is even more astonishing that these young churches have produced so many leaders who are able to take part on terms of equality in the development of the world-wide movement of the Christian churches. We may think of such men as D. T. Niles of Ceylon, chairman of the Youth Department of the World Council of Churches, a speaker and writer of unusual power; of Dr. P. D. Devanandan, literature secretary of the Y.M.C.A. and a contributor to the preparatory volumes for the first Assembly of the World Council of Churches in 1948; of Dr. D. G. Moses of Hislop College, Nagpur, a philosopher and a chosen speaker at the International Missionary Conferences held at Whitby in 1947 and Willingen in 1952.

But while we recognize and thank God for all this, it is important not to exaggerate, and to remember the other side, the real and grave weaknesses of the churches in the three countries.

A recent book by an Indian Christian layman, Mr. Rajaiah D. Paul, contains a chapter that no missionary and no Western visitor would have dared to write, on "Failures of the Indian Church."[1] The writer, who has had a long and distinguished career as a government servant, stands sufficiently apart from the church to view it objectively but sufficiently within it to write not as a mere critic but as a member of the church, deeply concerned about its future.

After noting various minor imperfections, Mr. Paul ends his survey by indicating two central weaknesses in the life of the church in his country.

The first great defect is that the Indian churches as a whole are not sufficiently moved by evangelistic zeal.

Indian Christians have not yet realized that it is personal evangelism and personal witnessing by Christian living that can win people over to Christianity. "Every baptized Christian a missionary" was the slogan that Bishop Azariah inculcated in the mind of his flock. But this cannot be said to be true of the vast majority of our churches. Even today active evangelistic work is being carried on mainly under the auspices of missions rather than by the church itself. The two great needs of the Indian church at the present time are that the people should feel their responsibility for the evangelization of their country and for giving liberally and sacrificially for the support of God's work.[2]

The second criticism is even more serious; it is that

[1] *The Cross over India*, by Rajaiah D. Paul, pp. 103-12. London, SCM Press, Ltd., 1952. Used by permission.

[2] *Ibid.*, pp. 110-11. Used by permission.

the Indian churches have lost their first love and have entered a period of spiritual doldrums:

> Except in certain limited areas where spiritual leadership has been exceptionally strong, Indian Christianity has lost its original freshness and zeal, and especially in areas where Christianity has been established long enough to become merely traditional and physically inherited the story of Indian Christianity is one of increasing degeneration in spirituality, though of progressive advancement in economic and cultural life. . . . From a worldly point of view we of the present generation are far better off than were our grandfathers and great-grandfathers, but from the spiritual point of view it must be admitted that Indian Christianity has lost all round. It should now be the endeavor of everyone interested in the Indian church to help us to recapture the simple faith, the fervent spirituality, the plainly visible power and the apostolic passion for souls which characterized the lives of our forefathers in what may well be called the apostolic age of Indian Christianity.[1]

Everyone who knows India will immediately be able to think of many exceptions to Mr. Paul's generalizations. Some of them have been plainly indicated in this chapter. But there is enough truth in them to give cause for anxiety. The Indian churches are faced with a new challenge and a great new opportunity. Will they rise to the height of that opportunity? The answer to this question depends on the way in which these churches gird themselves to face one by one the problems of the hour, and on a rediscovery of those unfailing sources of renewal that are to be found in Jesus Christ, the Way, the Truth and the Life.

[1] *Ibid.*, pp. 111-12. Used by permission.

4

Old Tasks in a New Setting

CHRISTIANS IN A NATIONAL EMERGENCY

Before independence, many Christians in India, both Indian and foreign, viewed the future with considerable apprehension. British administration had never been particularly friendly to missions, indeed, in its anxiety to be strictly impartial had not infrequently fallen over on the other side and done less than justice to the Christian cause. Nevertheless, it had maintained order and religious liberty; could it reasonably be hoped that the governments that would succeed to it would do the same?

In spite of these fears, when independence actually arrived, it came to most Christians as a relief and a new hope.

During the later years of the political struggle, missionaries were often told, even by their Indian Christian colleagues, who ought to have known better, that they were really though perhaps unconsciously agents of Western imperialism. If this had been true, it might have been supposed that, when Western imperialism came to an end, the missionaries would have resigned their work and gone home. Nothing of the kind happened. As far as I know, there is not a single example on record of any missionary of any nation or church resigning his work in India on political grounds. All the missionaries, whatever their political views, calmly accepted the new situation and went on with their work, after taking just one day's holiday on Independence Day itself.

Similarly, Indian Christians, a great many of whom had Western friends and, as Christians, had a far deeper understanding of the West than any non-Christian can have, had to bear the reproach, usually most unfair, of being only half-Indian and of being indifferent to their country's cause. To all of these the changed relations to Britain came as a great release. Now they could stand forth as citizens of their own country, with as good a claim as anybody else and without qualification; they could show themselves as loyal and devoted as the adherents of any other religion.

No sooner had independence been won than Christians had a unique opportunity to prove their worth and the central position that they hold in the community. From August 13 to November 15, 1947, as we have already recorded, terror descended on the whole frontier area between India and West Pakistan. Worse even than the loss of life and destruction of property was the embittered hostility and suspicion between the communities. In the disturbed areas no Hindu or Sikh trusted any Muslim, and in reverse no Muslim trusted any Hindu or Sikh. So deep was this distrust that it was impossible for men of good will in one community to serve those of another who were in desperate need. Christians, as the only genuine neutrals, had an unparalleled opportunity for disinterested service.

Governments did what they could, but their resources were soon exhausted. At this point the National Christian Council stepped into the breach. No less a person than Mr. Gandhi himself advised the Minister for Health in India to make contact with the council, assuring her that it was likely to have doctors and nurses available. Later, when the services rendered by Christians brought them under threats and danger from violent elements in the population, Mr. Gandhi issued a public statement, condemning the inhuman behavior of fanatics toward the Christians and exhorting the Christians to continue their splendid service, unmindful of what people said or did.

Christian medical units from West Pakistan traveled far into India to serve in the refugee camps for Muslims that had been established by the government of India. Conversely, teams from India penetrated into Pakistan to serve among Hindu and Sikh refugees. Many volunteers came forward to help the medical staffs.

In Purana Qila, the largest refugee camp for Muslims, and in Humayun's Tomb over 200 young Christian men and women worked with marvelous devotion and sacrifice. They looked after the sick, the wounded, and the maternity cases literally night and day, often without food and water, in heavy rain and hailstorms. Those who watched the youth work in a true Christ-like spirit thanked God for the marvel of his grace. The girls from the Y.W.C.A. need a special mention for their most selfless service.[1]

[1] *Do Unto Others* (a statement issued by the National Christian Council of India in 1950), p. 5. Throughout this section, I am much indebted to this clear and full account of relief work.

After the first wave of disasters and panic had subsided, there was much to do in the way of after care and rehabilitation. The interdenominational relief agency, Church World Service, immediately flew in supplies of the drugs most urgently needed, and these were followed by consignments of food and clothes. Recreation and welfare were not neglected. In the permanent refugee camps, activities included nursery schools, knitting classes, and worship. Phonographs and films were called in to help with the long, unoccupied hours that are the bane of refugee life. No attempt was made to make capital of distress for propaganda purposes; yet inevitably many among those who had received this loving service were ready to hear the message of the Saviour in whose name this work of mercy had been carried on.

Gradually needs became less, and governments found means to take over the responsibilities. But what the Christians had done in the emergency will never be forgotten, and never again should the suggestion be made that Christians are in some way second class citizens.

The agony of strife once mitigated, Christians were able to stand back and consider what their new situation in the independent countries actually was. In general, the results of this survey have been reassuring.

CHRISTIANITY AND THREE FLAGS

¶ India desires to take its stand as a secular, democratic republic. But the authorities have been anxious to make it clear that the word "secular" in this connection does not imply hostility to religion. On the contrary, it is recognized that the spiritual foundations of a nation's life are all important. But it is not the business of the state itself to support or propagate religion and, while impartial as between the adherents of all religions, it should not give special support or advantages to any. Under Christian influence, the Constituent Assembly included in the Constitution of India, as among the essential freedoms to which every citizen is entitled, the right to "profess, to practice, and to propagate" the religion of his choice. In the debate on this subject on December 6, 1948, some delegates objected to the inclusion of the term "propagate," but this view was not upheld by the majority. For instance, Mr. K. M. Munshi, a Hindu and a minister in the first cabinet of independent India, affirmed that:

In the old regime Christian missionaries might be said to have had an advantage, but in the present setup of a secular state there was no particular advantage provided for any one religion. He also refuted the suggestion that the Christian community were proselytizing. They wanted the retention of this right, not with any aggressive design of conversion, but because it was part of their religious injunction to propagate. Furthermore, under the right of free speech, expression, and association, the right to propagate one's religion was already guaranteed.

It would be hard to imagine a more specific charter of liberty for the Christian enterprise in India.

There is much evidence that the chief authorities in India take seriously this duty of religious impartiality. The prime minister, Mr. Nehru, has again and again inveighed against every kind of discrimination. Leaders have spoken in the warmest terms of the work of missionaries in the past. For instance, Dr. Lakshmanaswami

Mudaliar, vice-chancellor of the University of Madras, speaking on December 13, 1951, remarked that:

The good work done by the missionaries in India in all aspects of life was unforgettable. The service of the missionaries was unforgettable in its spontaneity, in its personal interest, and in its magnanimity. . . . It is that spirit that is required in the modern setup of our country, a spirit which inculcates the same missionary zeal, enthusiasm, devotion, and a strict sense of discipline in the minds of the taught.[1]

This is not to say that there have not been troubles and anxieties for the Christian community.

One of the most serious concerned the attitude of the government to those from the scheduled castes (that is, of those castes listed by the government as backward economically or in other ways, and especially in need of help) who had become Christians. In 1950 the President of the Republic issued an order, stating that only those members of the scheduled castes who professed Hinduism would be eligible for state aid. This was immediately and successfully challenged by Christians. A further statement was issued, affirming that it was only in regard to certain political rights, such as separate representation, that distinction could be made between different groups of backward people. A later government order laid it down that:

All state aid and facilities are to be given not only to the members of the Hindu scheduled castes but and equally to all other educationally and socially backward classes, whether they profess Hinduism, Sikhism, Christianity, or

[1] *The Guardian* (Madras), Dec. 20, 1951, p. 552.

any other religion. No distinction is to be made in this regard between Hindu scheduled castes and backward classes.

Finally, an amendment to the Constitution made it clear that discrimination against any religious community was not the policy of the government.

It has been laid down by government that ordinarily new missionaries would be allowed to enter to replace others or to augment the strength of the mission, "provided the need for such replacement or augmentation is established," and provided "that there is no suitable Indian available." [1]

In many areas, Christian instruction in schools can be given only to pupils whose parents specifically ask for it and then only out of school hours, a requirement that cannot be judged to be unreasonable, though it may make the religious work of schools in some places more difficult than it was under the old regime. More serious was the attempt of the government in Travancore and Cochin to insist that appointments of staff to a Christian school must be made only from an approved list of candidates maintained by the government department of education. This might have made difficult the replacement of Christians by other Christians. Happily, a compromise was reached that satisfied the desire of the government to insure that only qualified teachers were appointed and the need of the schools to retain reasonable liberty in the choice of staff.

A rather more serious situation was created in one state when the Surgeon general laid it down as a condition for further government support for a hospital that:

[1] Quoted by John W. Sadiq, "Church and State in India," in *International Review of Missions*, July, 1951, p. 293. Used by permission.

Future recruitments and also admission of patients at the center should be made from all communities alike, irrespective of their religion or race.

No proselytism should be carried on among the members of the staff and patients.[1]

These and other similar events are a warning to the churches that they must not in future count on such unrestricted liberty as they enjoyed in the British period.

Some recent discussions, especially on the subject of direct evangelistic work by missionaries and "proselytism," have indicated a hardening of the official Indian attitude and possibly a growing anti-Christian feeling in the country. These utterances should serve as a warning to the Indian church that it should put its house in order and take now such steps as are necessary to insure the carrying on of its work, if a time comes when missionary help is no longer available and government aid is entirely withdrawn from its institutions. But so far nothing has happened radically to change the relation of churches to governments or to interfere with the unbroken continuity of Christian work.

The situation in Pakistan is slightly different. Pakistan came into existence through the determination of the Muslims to free themselves from Hindu control and to create a new state on an Islamic pattern. Leaders have proclaimed again and again that Pakistan is to be an Islamic state; yet at the same time they have affirmed that its guiding principles are to be democracy, freedom, equality, tolerance, and social justice, without any clear definition of how these ideas, which seem to be mutually exclusive, are to be reconciled. When the Committee

[1] Quoted by Sadiq, *op. cit.*, p. 294. Used by permission.

of the Constituent Assembly on Fundamental Rights issued its recommendations, they were immediately challenged by thirty-one leaders of Muslim thought in Pakistan as inconsistent with Islam.

The leading figures in the present government are, it is clear, modernized Muslims who close their eyes to the fact that, as long as the Koran and *Sunna* are legalistically invoked as the basis of the life of the state, any attempt to construct a modern democratic state can be made only on a foundation of medieval principles and patterns. . . . They stubbornly overlook this essential fact and escape into the assertion of general principles, which are labelled Islamic but are really the product of secularized Western political thought. The most pathetic feature in the whole situation is that they extol Islam without having any real religious attachment to it. There is no realization that to mold a state on an Islamic basis presupposes a religious and moral revival and that it cannot be done by enunciating principles which spring from the head instead of the heart.[1]

It is clear that the higher authorities in Pakistan accept the principle of the equality of all communities, as affirmed in the document *Fundamental Rights of Pakistan Citizens*, and are doing their best to prevent any discrimination. In 1951, at a Christian convention held at Gujranwala, the Minister for Rehabilitation of the government of Western Punjab assured his hearers that Christians and Muslims enjoyed equal rights as citizens of Pakistan and that the government was doing everything in its power to bring comfort and prosperity to the Christians who had chosen to make their homes in

[1] "On Tour through Southeast Asia," by Hendrik Kraemer, in *The Ecumenical Review*, January, 1952, p. 119. Used by permission. The whole passage, pp. 117-21, is a most incisive discussion of the paradox of Pakistan.

Pakistan. He warned them against thinking that the careless action of some local officer represented the considered policy of the government.[1]

This is not, however, to say that there are not many inconveniences and harassing problems for a Christian community living under predominantly Muslim rule.

It is reported that, in spite of theoretical equality, Christians find it difficult to enter government service, either in the civil or the military department, that all key positions are held by Muslims, and that employment in commercial firms and businesses is not readily open to Christians.

No pupil in a school in Pakistan can be graduated without having passed an examination in religious knowledge. At the start the government insisted that in all schools receiving help from the government the Koran must be read and studied, an obligation that many Christian schools found it impossible conscientiously to fulfill. Now the order has been changed; Christian schools are not obliged to teach the Koran, and it is regarded as sufficient if Muslim pupils are given free time in which to pursue their Islamic studies at the local mosque.[2]

However, a recent resolution of the Christian Council of East Pakistan indicates a difficulty that is not likely so soon to disappear. The resolution is to the effect that all Christian children should, where necessary, attend day school on Sunday and take their examinations on that day, still doing their best by attendance at Sunday school and church services before and after school to fulfill their religious duties. The Muslim holy day is

[1] *Ecumenical Press Service* (N. Y. C.), November 28, 1951, p. 4.
[2] *Eglise Vivante*, 1952, no. 2, p. 242.

Friday. In the British period Sunday was the usual holiday, though Muslim schools sometimes worked on Sunday when this was necessary in order to make up for
working days lost through Muslim festivals. Now in a
Muslim state Friday naturally takes precedence over
Sunday, and this resolution was necessary to give guid-
ance to pupils and parents, whose consciences were
troubled by the necessity of infringing the traditional
Christian use of Sunday.[1]

Much more serious, however, than any such minor
inconveniences is the general economic situation of the
church in West Pakistan. Christians in that area have always been poor, but the dislocation and confusion
caused by the mass migrations have made their condition far worse than it was before. It has recently been
stated by an expert that Christians in West Pakistan are
"displaced persons in their own country." Many of
them are refugees who have fled from India. Others
find themselves out of a job, since the new Muslim
owners of the soil no longer require the services that the
Christians used to render to the former Hindu land-
lords. Almost all are farmers, passionately attached to
the land and with no idea of making their living in any
other way.

The first measures for the relief of distress have had
their effects, and what is needed now is a long term
economic policy having sufficient aid from outside to
make it workable, with a view to putting the Christian
community firmly on its feet and enabling it to play
an independent part in the life of the community as a
whole. Of course such a program cannot take the place

[1] *South India Churchman*, June, 1952, p. 13.

of spiritual upbuilding, but all recent studies show that spiritual upbuilding tends to fail of its effects unless it is accompanied by such care for the whole man as is implied in concern for economic development as well. Such a program would have to be carried on under four aspects:

1. As many Christians as possible should be settled on land sufficient to maintain them in reasonable comfort. The government has assigned certain lands, but not all of them are suitable or cultivable. In many places, capital expenditure is needed for deep boring of wells or other irrigation projects, and for this financial help will be needed from the West.

2. As it is impossible that all Christians be provided with land, development of small industries, such as tanning and leatherwork, as an alternative means of livelihood is essential. Unfortunately, few Christians at present have enough skill to run such businesses and to make them pay, and those brought up on the land do not easily turn to other types of work.

3. The extreme poverty of the Christians is hindering the spread of education among them. Scholarships are needed to make sure that a sufficient number of Christian young people are trained to be leaders among their own folk later on.

4. Since young men are already beginning to drift into the towns in search of work, a special service is needed to help them find jobs and to guard them against the dangers of sinking to the level of the rootless proletariat, which would make them susceptible to Communist propaganda.

This is a formidable program. It is clear that the Pakistani church and the missionary societies together will have their hands full for as far into the future as is foreseeable. Realism demands that the gloomier elements in the situation be faced without evasion. But happily, this is not the whole picture. Not long ago it was possible for a former Moderator of the United Church of Northern India to write that "the church in Pakistan, in spite of certain handicaps, seems to be much more alive to the great evangelistic opportunity today than ever before." [1]

Encouraging reports have been received of renewed evangelistic activity. In November, 1952, a group touring with a book van of the Bible Society visited over thirty villages and was able to preach and sell books in almost every place with little opposition. As a result of this witness, the inhabitants of several villages have asked for further instruction in the Christian way.

Certain inconveniences and certain threats of worse things to come only emphasize the general tolerance that the church in the three countries enjoys and the freedom with which Christian work can be carried on. What use will the churches make of this freedom that for the moment is theirs, and what are the new tasks to which they are called in the mid-twentieth century?

THE WORK OF THE CHURCH

¶ The first and continuing task is that of making the gospel known through the length and breadth of the territories.

Missionary work has been carried on so long, and with

---

[1] *National Christian Council Review*, Jan., 1953, p. 19. Used by permission.

such success, that there is a general impression in the West that India as a whole has been reached by the gospel, that the day of the pioneer is over, and that all that is needed now is the strengthening and building up of the church. A brief study of the facts and of the map will make it clear that this is not so, and that India, Pakistan, and Ceylon are still largely unevangelized countries. It is true that the church has been spreading and growing and that the areas in which there is no Christian witness of any kind are fewer than they were, but they still exist, and there are far more areas in which the Christian witness is so sparse and rare as hardly to make any impression at all on the mass of the population. A few specific instances will help to make this clear.

In Rajasthan is the state of Tonk, with an area slightly larger than that of the state of Delaware and with a comparable population. The *Directory of Churches and Missions* for 1951 gives the number of Christians in Tonk as 21, and sums up the condition of Christian work and witness by the laconic word *nil*. Is there any Christian reason why Delaware should be so much more highly favored than Tonk?

Four contiguous districts in Uttar Pradesh have an area rather larger than that of Connecticut and a population of more than 3 million. In the whole area, there are slightly more than 5,000 Christians, served by five ordained ministers and four other Christian workers. What are the figures for Connecticut, and is Connecticut in some way dearer to God than Uttar Pradesh?

The independence of India has opened to the church many doors that were formerly closed. Under British administration, the rulers of the independent Indian states had the right to determine whether they would or would not allow Christian preaching in their dominions. Many of them kept their states firmly shut against all Christian penetration. One of the largest such areas was the state of Rewa in Central India, which has an area nearly as large as that of Maryland and a population of over two million. This was one of the most backward areas in India; 98 per cent of the population was illiterate, and social services hardly existed. Sick people used to come over the border to be treated at the Anglican mission hospital at Mirzapur, but there was no way to follow up the patients in their own homes. A small Indian Lutheran mission was working just beyond the southeastern border of the state. Now the restrictions have been swept away, as the provisions of the Indian constitution for religious liberty hold sway also in this area. A small Lutheran group, not more than five or six strong, has been able to cross the border and enter Rewa. But how many churches and ministers are regarded as necessary for the evangelization and spiritual care of Maryland?

Ultimately evangelization must be the responsibility of the church in India, Pakistan, and Ceylon. But if the church is to fulfill this task, it must be a church renewed, purified, filled with the Holy Spirit, and able to stand firmly on its own feet. A sense of special urgency has been created in the minds of all thoughtful Christians in India by what has recently happened in China. Suppose that the church of India were to pass through a similar ordeal, were to be separated entirely from contact and fellowship with the West and subjected to the strain of ceaseless Communist propaganda and intimidation. How would it show itself under such testing—this church so sorely divided within itself, still so largely foreign in leadership, still so largely dependent on foreign money, still so undeveloped in regard to its own inner resources and potentialities? Would it survive and grow, or would it be reduced to impotence? These are much more than academic questions.

TRAINED LEADERSHIP

¶ On one point almost all are agreed—that the immediate task is to secure more adequate training for the Indian leadership of the church.

In 1938 the International Missionary Conference held at Tambaram near Madras expressed the judgment that, of all the possible forms of missionary work, none was more important than the training of the ministry of the church and that none was being less effectively carried on. India took the hint. A strong committee was appointed, and a survey was made of all the training at that time being carried on in (undivided) India. The results were set forth in a very able book, *The Christian Minister in India*, by Dr. Charles W. Ranson,[1] now general secretary of the International Missionary Council. And then things began to happen.

The center of theological training for the whole of India is the great college founded at Serampore on the banks of the Hooghly in 1818 by Carey and his colleagues. Serampore was at that time a Danish colony, and the college still retains the privilege, accorded to it by the King of Denmark in its charter and unique in

[1] National Christian Council of India, Burma, and Ceylon, 1946.

India, of giving theological degrees. Students from all over the subcontinent and beyond earn the B.D. degree of Serampore. The college was founded by Baptists and for more than a century was a Baptist institution, though welcoming students from many churches. Now, however, it is a union institution, depending on the support of several institutions and churches. A new stage in development was marked by the appointment of its first Indian principal, Dr. C. E. Abraham, a priest of the Mar Thoma Syrian Church of Travancore.

Around Serampore are grouped several other colleges, among them the Anglican Bishop's College, Calcutta, and Leonard Theological College, Jabalpur, founded by the Methodists, which cater to students who already have a degree in arts or sciences and which offer courses entirely in English. This is inevitable, since in such colleges the students are drawn from many language areas and have no common Indian language. The use of English presents also the advantage of introducing students directly to the treasures of Western theological literature. It has, however, certain drawbacks. It does not always follow that the student can reproduce in his own language what he has learned in English. One of the ablest Indian Christian leaders, the Brahman convert, Paul Ramaseshan, whose death in 1951 was a loss to the whole Indian church, told the writer that when he left the theological college and took up his ministry he found it necessary to write his sermons in English and then laboriously translate them into Tamil, his own language. So strong was the hold of English and so strong the conviction even of Indians that theological instruction could be given in an Indian language only on a lower and elementary level, that English had been generally adopted as the medium of instruction even in theological schools where the students were not college graduates and where all came from a single language area.

The Ranson report raised again the question whether the time had not come to develop the resources of the Indian languages and courageously to use them as the vehicle for higher theological teaching.

For a number of years theological lectures had been given in Tamil at Tirumaraiyur, "the village of the holy revelation," in the theological school of the Anglican diocese of Tinnevelly in the far south. Tamil, spoken by 25 million people, has a great classical literature dating back to at latest the second century of the Christian era. It is a rich and flexible form of human speech. Very little difficulty was experienced in adapting it to theological purposes. In 1951, Tirumaraiyur was adopted as the united theological college of the Church of South India for the whole Tamil area, with a Christian constituency of about 400,000, and Tamil was accepted as the main medium of instruction.

Now, Tirumaraiyur does not stand alone. The Kerala United Theological Seminary for the Malayalam speaking area of the southwest; Union Theological Seminary, Indore, for the Hindi-speaking region; the United Theological College of Western India at Poona (Marathi-speaking) draw together the efforts and the students of a number of churches, on the basis of using and developing Indian languages as the means for the expression of the full range of Christian truth. The rate at which this can be done depends on the flexibility of the languages themselves and on the production of the necessary Christian literature in them.

No need in India is greater than that for doctors. At present there is only one qualified doctor for every 6,000 of the population, and even this low figure has been attained only as a result of rapid progress during this century. There is a specific Christian attitude to the work of healing, involving certain standards of integrity, respect for the personality of the sufferer, and recognition of the spiritual as a vital factor even in professional competence, which is difficult to acquire in the secular atmosphere of a government institution. The great union Christian Medical College at Vellore is the fruit of the conviction that Christian doctors can be trained only in Christian surroundings.

Like most great achievements, Vellore has grown from very small beginnings. It all began when Ida Scudder, a granddaughter of the first American medical missionary in India, felt the call to medical missionary service. In 1900, Dr. Scudder started work in a single room in her father's house. In 1918, with extraordinary faith and courage, she started a medical school for women, at a time when women graduates were very few and the Indian woman doctor was almost unknown. In 1947 men students were admitted, and the college now serves the whole Indian church, offering full courses for the degree of M.B., B.S. of the University of Madras, and for the degree of B.Sc. in nursing of the same university.

What gives Vellore its special character is that it is one of the most genuinely ecumenical enterprises in the whole world. It is supported by forty church and mission bodies, and the staff is drawn from India, the United States, Canada, Great Britain, Ireland, Australia, Germany, and Switzerland. Under its distinguished Indian director, Dr. Hilda Lazarus, it combines in a wonderful way care for men's bodies and for their spirits:

> The chapels at both college and hospital are central not only in situation but in their significance. Morning and evening prayers are held daily in both, and the Sunday evening services are an important feature of the week. Evangelism in the hospital and surrounding villages is carried on under the direction of a full time chaplain by means of daily ward prayers, lantern talks, and the distribution of Gospels and tracts. Weekly Bible classes for all students are conducted by members of the staff.[1]

What Vellore has been to the south, Ludhiana has been to the north. What Dr. Ida Scudder has been to Vellore, Dame Edith Brown has been to Ludhiana. Ludhiana stands on the same broad ecumenical base as "an interdenominational college existing for the benefit of all Protestant missionary bodies and churches in India, to train doctors, nurses, dispensers, midwives." [2] Like Vellore, this college has raised the large sums necessary to provide the full graduate course in medicine and surgery, and thus to produce doctors who can hold their own on equal status with those who have studied in the government medical colleges.

The training of professional leadership for the church is of the greatest importance. But the Indian churches

---

[1] *Christian Medical College, Vellore, South India.* Madras, 1951, p. 10.

[2] *Directory of Churches and Missions in India and Pakistan, 1951,* p. 312.

have not been unaffected by the ecumenical current, which brings into the center of the picture of the church's life the layman in his work and witness.

LAY FOLK TAKE A HAND

¶ Most of the churches in the three countries are democratically organized; thousands of lay men and women play their part in committees and councils and are learning to take great decisions (such as those affecting the unity of the church) in a spirit of prudence and Christian wisdom.

As we have seen, the pillar of the Indian church is the unordained village worker, the schoolteacher who is also lay preacher.

It is impossible to overestimate the service rendered to the church by the typical village teacher, whom we shall call John Devasahayam (divine help), and his like minded wife Kirubai (grace). The two together run a village school, covering the first five years of education. John conducts Sunday services, except on the one Sunday in the month when the ordained pastor is present for the sacramental ministrations of the church. He takes evening prayers every day (the bell ringing at sundown for evening worship is one of the most characteristic sounds of the Indian Christian village). His house is open at all hours to all comers. It is his task to guide and advise his little flock in their problems, to provide first aid when they are sick, to reconcile them when they quarrel, to represent them in their relations with their non-Christian neighbors and the government, to lead them in their evangelistic enterprises. His wife conducts the women's fellowship and the Sunday school.

With slender theological qualifications and a library containing less than a dozen books, he must carry on in isolation and loneliness, in good times and in bad, in cheer and in discouragement, undeterred by criticism and opposition. It is not surprising that sometimes his spiritual resources fail and his energy runs down. The village worker will not appear at ecumenical conferences, but his record is written in heaven, and the Indian church is largely his creation.

But it is just at this point that the work of the churches is most vulnerable. The wide extension of the teacher-catechist system was made possible only by government grants-in-aid to Christian schools. But supposing that the government were to lay down conditions such as would make the maintenance of Christian schools impossible, or were to decide to nationalize education and to undertake it all itself. How would the church then be able to maintain the structure of its village work?

Farsighted leaders have long seen that the church must begin now to prepare for this revolution. It has been noticed that among the churches that grow most rapidly in the East are those that, like the Pentecostal groups, have no paid nor ordained ministry and rely on the working of the Spirit of God in the ordinary members of the congregation. Is there not here perhaps a lesson that the older and more rigidly organized churches should learn?

The diocese of Madura and Ramnad of the South India church decided to take steps to train lay people for spiritual responsibility in villages where there is no school and no paid worker and to prepare in advance for the day, if it comes, when the paid worker in the village will no longer exist. The first plan was to bring lay leaders in to the seminary at Pasumalai for a month of study. This was hardly successful. Very few farmers, even in the slack season, can leave their fields for a whole month; even those who made the sacrifice and did so found that their minds were constantly divided between attention to the teaching and anxiety about the state of the crops at home. The new experiment is to make the training peripatetic, by holding week-end training courses in a number of centers. These have proved immediately popular and have gathered eager groups of students under conditions as little removed as possible from their ordinary way of life. An occasional week end of study may not seem an adequate substitute for four years of seminary training, but who shall despise the day of small things? For the simple village folk, these simple witnesses may be more effective than a seminary graduate weighed down with an excess of academic learning.

In missionary work it is hard to find anything that can be regarded as an absolutely new beginning, but one enterprise of young lay people has recently been recorded that may be regarded as a quite new contribution to the life of the Indian church. All over the world, young people are finding that a natural expression of their spiritual yearning to build a new world is found in the international Christian work camp, where young people of many nations gather to work hard and long on some project concerned with the advancement of the cause of Christ in the world.

Recently the Assam Christian Council decided that Assam must have a Christian college of its own. There was a fine project but little money. A group of educated young Christians offered their services for nearly a month in October, 1951, to do with their own hands the preliminary work of clearing and preparing the site. In India it is not the custom for educated folk to dirty their hands with hard manual toil; such work is for the coolie and not for the student. Mr. Gandhi to some extent broke through this age old prejudice by his insistence on hand spinning as an obligation for every member of the Congress Party—but spinning is a tame occupation compared with clearing jungle. It is this breach with tradition that makes the efforts of these young people so eloquent and so moving.

When the campers reached the site, they found plenty of land—fifteen hundred acres of it. But there, where God willing a lovely Christian college will one day stand, the campers did not find even a single building. Only a wilderness waiting to be conquered. The wilderness was thickly covered with *lantana* bushes, bearing beautiful yellow and orange flowers, but with roots tough enough to rope an elephant. The weeks resolved themselves largely into a struggle between human muscles and *lantana* roots.

Hard work, under any circumstances. If you don't think so, try it next time you see a *lantana* bush. But the real test came when the drizzling rain caught us only ten minutes after reaching the job. As everyone got wetter and wetter, the directors suggested that the students might want to go back to camp. Nothing doing! They had come to work, and a little thing like rain was not going to stop them. . . . The campers felt like the children of Israel going up to take possession of the Promised Land. Each day, before setting off for work, they formed a circle, holding their hoes, axes, big knives, crowbars, and ropes. There they would bow their heads to ask God's blessing on all their work, nor did they become too engrossed in their labors ever to forget that they were co-workers with him in a great venture of faith. The "giants in the land"—difficult working conditions, fear that enough of the task would not be completed, worry about the ultimate success or failure of the college itself—seemed to dwindle away when someone would start up a song, or when all turned to God once more in prayer.[1]

If there is one place more than any other in which the witness of Christian lay folk is vital to the well-being of the church, it is the Christian home, the essential unit of the larger family of God. On February 10, 1949, the Executive Committee of the World Council of Churches, considering the perils by which the church is faced where communism takes charge, laid it down that:

The life of every individual Christian and of every Christian family must be so rooted in Christ that the faith lives on, even though the church for a period be deprived of every earthly protection, broken into fragments, and stripped of everything except its fellowship with its Lord.[2]

Although their situation at the moment is comfortable enough, this is a warning that the Indian churches might well heed. There is much that is beautiful in Indian family life. The ideal of the perfect Indian wife was set for all time in the figure of Sita in the great Indian epic the *Ramayana*. The intense affection, not always tempered by wisdom, of Indian parents for their children is a joy to behold. But for the most part the position

[1] *Youth News* (National Christian Council of India), Feb., 1952, pp. 20-21. Used by permission.
[2] *Ecumenical Press Service*, Feb. 11, 1949, p. 45.

of the woman has been subordinate, and the Christian idea of mutual respect and equality in the service of the Lord is one of the newest and best gifts that the gospel has to offer to India. The Christian home is a new creation. But it was plain that a vast multitude of Christian homes fell far short of the ideal, and that this was a point at which the renewal of the church was urgently needed.

In January, 1941, the National Christian Council convened a conference to consider the inauguration of a united effort to stress the ideals and meet the problems of Christian home and family life in India. The result has been the inauguration of the Christian Home Festival, now in many areas one of the most notable events in the Christian year. The nature of the celebration varies much from place to place, but usually there is instruction in baby care, family devotions, gardening, sanitation, and recreation.

In one village special meetings were held throughout a week. One evening families were invited to present original ten minute plays on some aspect of family life, and they revealed unsuspected talent. "In one case a small girl tried to eat unripe mangoes, despite her father's admonition as to the vitamin value of spinach. In another there was an earnest effort to balance the budget while insistent voices demanded hair ribbons and kites!" At the concluding service, the head of each family made his vow, "As for me and my house, we will serve the Lord," and then all together repeated the simple charter of the Christian home:

> Christ is the Light of the world
> Christ is the Light of our home
> Christ is the Light of *my* life.

It is reported that the results of the observance of the festival have been amazing. "Broken families have been reunited, discipline in homes changed from beating and cursing to gentle and constructive ways." [1]

REACTIONS TO THE WESTERN IMPACT

¶ The aim of renewal in the church is witness. Christian witness has to be carried on in changed conditions and adapted to them. The cardinal new factor today is the revival of the three great classical religions of the subcontinent, Hinduism, Buddhism, and Islam. Each has passed through a period of crisis and temporary decline, but today each seems to be gathering together its inner strength and to be entering a period of aggressive activity.

When British supremacy was finally established in India, the impact of Western thought and Western ways on its age old life came to be felt as overwhelming. When the first dust began to clear, it soon became evident that this tremendous impact was being met by three reactions.

There was first the reaction of total acceptance. The middle of the nineteenth century was the time when Indian gentlemen wore formal European dress under the tropic sun and were proud of the fact that, while they talked English with Augustan grace, they could not express themselves in any Indian dialect. One aspect of this reaction of acceptance was the small but steady stream of high caste converts to Christianity, who laid

[1] Quotations throughout the two preceding paragraphs are from "Six Forms of Work," by John W. Sadiq, in *World Christian Education, Fourth Quarter*, 1952, p. 85. Used by permission.

the foundation of most of the famous Indian Christian families, a stream that began steadily to dry up in about 1870.

Then there was the reaction of total rejection. Many Hindus withdrew into the fastnesses of the old ways, refused all contact with the alien, and maintained as god-given every feature of Hindu practice, including untouchability and child marriage. It is only in the light of this conservative reaction that the assassination of Mr. Gandhi becomes understandable.

The third solution was that of synthesis. The Hindu claimed the right to accept that which pleased him in Western civilization and Christian faith and to work out strange new combinations of the inheritances of East and West. This involved a rediscovery of the pure and noble elements in the ancient Hindu Scriptures, especially the *Upanishads* and the *Bhagavad-Gita*, but also an openness to new ideas, whatever their source, and particularly to the ideas of the Christian gospel. To the Hindu such syncretism is not illogical, since, as Dr. Paul D. Devanandan explains to us, he is convinced that the Ultimate Reality remains essentially unknowable, all religions are partially true but none is wholly true, and that "if one accepts many different interpretations of God and Reality, believing in the essential truths for which they separately stand, the sum total of partial truths will certainly be more than the partial truth affirmed by any one religion." [1]

One of the greatest of syncretisers was Mr. Gandhi himself. His autobiography makes it clear that in early

[1] "Evangelism in a Renascent India," by Paul D. Devanandan, in *World Dominion*, Nov.-Dec., 1951, p. 342. Used by permission.

years in South Africa he was seriously considering becoming a Christian. He never took the decisive step, but
throughout his life he continued to be profoundly influenced by the teachings of Christ, though in later years
he made the affirmation that he found deeper values in
the Hindu *Bhagavad-Gita* than in the Christian Gospels.

Mr. Gandhi's influence on the Christian movement in
India was curiously contradictory. By his own reverence
for Jesus Christ and his teachings, he swept away the
previously prevailing attitude of hostility and distrust,
and encouraged literally millions of Hindus to read and
value the Gospels and to accept Jesus Christ as *one* of
the saviors of mankind. But equally by his example, he
encouraged them to believe that it was possible to ex-
tract and enjoy all the values of the Christian faith without such an exclusive loyalty to Christ as would be
expressed in joining the Christian church through baptism.

A more typical figure even than Mr. Gandhi is the
distinguished Indian philosopher, Dr. S. Radhakrishnan,
for some time Indian ambassador in Moscow and now
vice-president of the Indian Republic. According to Dr.
Radhakrishnan, Hinduism has already united a wide
range of beliefs and forms of worship in a loose federation united not "in a common creed but in a common
quest," and what it has done for India it might do for
the world, not by destroying other religions, but by
uniting them with itself in the quest after the Supreme
Reality, the inmost self of all spiritual being. Dr. Radhakrishnan finds it possible to unite with Christians in
worship, but he holds that in the first rank of seekers are
to be found only those who worship the Supreme Real-

ity as the impersonal Absolute. He relegates to the second rank those who believe in a personal God and to the third rank the worshipers of the incarnations. Pure classical Hinduism is therefore regarded as the highest of all forms of "the quest," and Christianity finds its place only in the second or third rank, as one of the inferior religions.[1]

The new confidence of Hinduism in itself has been given clear expression by Dr. Radhakrishnan in the following terms:

> After a long winter of some centuries, we are today in one of the creative periods of Hinduism. We are beginning to look upon our ancient faith with fresh eyes. Leaders of Hindu thought and practice are convinced that the times require, not a surrender of the basic principles of Hinduism, but a restatement of them with special reference to the need of a more complex and mobile social order.[2]

Perhaps the believers in a Hindu renaissance have underestimated the extent and the depth of the reconstruction that will be needed if Hinduism is to become once again the real motive power in the life of India. Traditionally Hinduism has been a world renouncing religion. The world and all that is in it is *maya*, illusion; in this world there is no possibility of any real achievement, and salvation is to be achieved by final and definitive escape from the world and from separate existence. Today there is a serious disharmony between these an-

[1] *The Hindu View of Life*, by S. Radhakrishnan. New York, The Macmillan Co., 1927. See also the admirable exposition by Dr. C. C. J. Webb, in *Journal of Theological Studies*, Oct., 1951.

[2] Quoted by Rajaiah D. Paul in *The Cross over India*, p. 117. London, SCM Press, Ltd., 1952. Used by permission.

cient beliefs and the way in which men live and act. India is surging with a spirit of renewal and new hope. Men believe that the socal order can be renewed, that the field of history is one in which self-sacrifice is worth while and in which real achievement is possible. Indians are convinced that they have a destiny to fulfill in the world of nations and a special contribution to make to the welfare of the world as a whole. Whether Hindu doctrine can be so expanded as to afford a valid basis for this activist ideal is a problem to which the future alone can give an answer.

The Western impact placed Islam under much the same difficulties as Hinduism. Muslims became aware that there was much in their faith and its social implications that was sharply criticized in the West and particularly in Christian circles. Over most of the Muslim world the reaction was that of stubborn assertion of the excellence of Islam and a refusal to consider the gospel impartially.

To this general attitude there have been outstanding exceptions in India. The first great Muslim leader who tried to show Muslims the way to a reconciliation of the old and the new was Sir Syed Ahmad Khan, who died in 1898, the founder of the Muslim University at Aligarh. Syed Ahmad Khan combined an enthusiastic welcome to Western science with the conviction that Islam could be restated in such a way as to give satisfaction to every modern need. His basic principle was that, although Islam is revelation, in the interpretation of it "reason alone is a sufficient guide." The great defense of Islam is to manifest its conformity with nature. "Islamic law provided the everyday ethic for every believer, while Christ offered an ideal for superior spirits." [1]

The mantle of Syed Ahmad Khan fell upon Sir Muhammad Iqbal, a great poet in the Urdu and Persian tongues, who until his death in 1939 was the outstanding leader in modern Islamic thought in India. In his *Six Lectures on the Reconstruction of Religious Thought in Islam,* he drew out afresh the program for the adaptation of Islam to the contemporary world.

With the reawakening of Islam, therefore, it is necessary to examine, in an independent spirit, what Europe has thought and how far the conclusions reached by her can help us in the revision and, if necessary, reconstruction, of theological thought in Islam. . . . The only course open to us is to approach modern knowledge with a respectful but independent attitude and to appreciate the teachings of Islam in the light of that knowledge, even though we may be led to differ from those who have gone before us.[2]

One of the cardinal points of the new Islam was the re-presentation given to the character of Mohammed himself.

The modernists stepped in and supplied a new image of Muhammad, by which the Christian attack was parried and the defense even turned into an offensive. . . . This new image . . . takes, one by one, all the cardinal virtues and presents Muhammad as embodying them in the highest degree. Not only is he made the exemplar of charity, purity,

[1] *India, Pakistan and the West,* by Percival Spear, p. 190. London, Oxford University Press, 1949. The whole chapter on "The Indian Response" is an admirable study of the subject under discussion.

[2] Quoted in *Modern Trends in Islam,* by H. A. R. Gibb, p. 76. Chicago, University of Chicago Press, copyright 1947. Used by permission.

truth, and all the rest, but the newer European ideologies provide a pedestal on which to exalt his manliness, his qualities of insight and leadership, and his revolutionary vigor.[1]

Islam had gathered its inner strength against the revolutionary shock of the West and of Christian preaching. The anxious Muslim world could breathe again.

The Muslim who accepted his religion from these writings might hold his head high, even when confronting Western Europe. His religion, point by point, is proved the finest in the world—judged by the most modern standards. The Prophet whom he adores is the supreme character of all history. The Muslim might well be proud and confident. The spirit of his religion, he found, is the highest liberal ideals, put here in contemporary and in glowing terms.[2]

Such ideas as these are widespread among educated Muslims today, and, combined with the contemporary sense of an Islamic mission to the whole world, underlie the political movement that led to the formation of Pakistan as an independent state. To the inner inconsistencies involved in this attitude we have already alluded. But ideas are not always effective only in proportion to their consistency. The Whitby Missionary Conference in 1947 drew attention to resurgent Islam as one of the three major hindrances to the spread of the gospel in the world.

Buddhism has died out in India, the country of its origin, but it is still the dominant religion of Ceylon. Like Hinduism and Islam, Buddhism has in recent years been experiencing a significant revival.

[1] *Ibid.*, p. 76. Used by permission.
[2] *Modern Islam in India*, by Wilfred Cantwell Smith, p. 56. Quoted in Gibb, *op. cit.*, p. 77.

There are several strands in the revival. There is a certain nostalgia for the past. Archaeology has revealed the greatness of the ancient Buddhist civilization in Ceylon. Just as Hindus in India are turning back to the ancient Hindu Scriptures for inspiration, so many Buddhists believe that a recovery of the pure spirit of the past may be the way to new greatness in the present. There is a sense of world mission. Ceylon was chosen as the scene of the first conference of the World Fellowship of Buddhists, which was held in Colombo from March 25 to June 6, 1950. Buddhists believe that their doctrine of quiescence and reverence for life is that which alone can give peace to the world. The Conference deliberately declared it as its aim that "when the twenty-five hundredth year after the passing away of the Buddha is reached in 1956, the whole world will have adopted the Buddhist way of life." But the movement is actuated in part by conscious hostility to the spread of Christianity.

The policy of the government of Ceylon is to support and encourage all religions equally. But there are various ways in which this policy can be turned to the disadvantage of one religion as against another. Complaint is made that the government has forced on Buddhists public holidays that mean nothing to them, an allusion to the general acceptance of Sunday as a holiday in Ceylon as in other countries that have come under Western influence. In schools, it is required that a pupil be taught only the religion of his parents or guardian, so that if Buddhist parents, or parents one of whom is Buddhist and the other Christian, desire that a child shall be taught the Christian faith, this freedom of choice is denied them by the law. In the University of Ceylon, Hinduism, Buddhism, and Islam are included in the curriculum in the department of Oriental Languages and Eastern Philosophy, but no provision is made for the teaching of Christianity, though it has been possible for the churches to erect a place of worship close to the university and to appoint a chaplain.

In imitation of Christian practice, hundreds of Buddhist Sunday schools have been started, with a graded system of examinations. In Buddhist periodicals, a steady anti-Christian campaign is being carried on.

On the national level, it is contended that Ceylon is the land of Buddhism and to be a Christian is to be untrue to the sacred duty of Ceylon. On the philosophical level, it is maintained that Buddhism is superior to Christianity, for it does not teach anything which is unverifiable by human experience, whereas Christianity is cumbered with so-called "revealed truth." On the religious level, Christianity is accused of debunking men by elevating God and thereby of sabotaging man's confidence in himself. On the moral level, the Buddhist ethic is extolled above the Christian because it teaches that all life is one and all forms of life must be treated with equal "compassion". . . . And on the social level, Christianity is accused of being a religion that does not condemn "drinking" and "gambling." [1]

The simultaneous revival and reconstruction of the ancient faiths presents Christian evangelism with new problems and new tasks. How is the new task to be accomplished?

[1] "Buddhist Ceylon," by D. T. Niles: in *World Dominion*, July-Aug., 1951, p. 220. Used by permission. The whole of this article is most valuable.

The first demand is for a profound study of these religions in their contemporary forms. "A center must be set up for the study of Buddhism and for keeping in touch with the Buddhist movement. Christian evangelists must read contemporary Buddhist writing, for how can we establish communication with minds of whose thinking we are ignorant?" [1]

In India this need has already to some extent been met by the foundation of the Henry Martyn School of Islamics and the Society for the Study of Hinduism, in both of which the modern situation and the modern approach to these religions are being carefully considered.

But there is the difficulty that most Christian scholars in the Asian churches are the children of Christian parents, and they, no less than the foreigners, approach the ancient religions as strangers from without. It has been noted that in the early days of the church its greatest defenders were men who had been converted in adult life. Among the Latins, Tertullian, Cyprian, Ambrose, and Augustine had all made careers for themselves as pagans before their conversion, all knew thoroughly and from within the life and thought of the ancient world. The churches should pray today for the conversion of such men in India, Pakistan, and Ceylon. In the early days of missions, there were such conversions. We should not regard them as impossible today. In the nineteenth century, the Indian church gave to the world two great Christian poets. One of these was H. A. Krishna Pillai, the author of a Tamil Christian epic based on the *Pilgrim's Progress*, one of whose lyrics is to be found in *Cantate Domino*, the international

[1] *Ibid.*, p. 222. Used by permission.

hymn book of the Student Christian Federation. The
other was Narayan Vaman Tilak, the Maratha Brahman, several of whose hymns have been translated and
are to be found in Western hymn books.[1] Both these
men were Hindu scholars, converted in the prime of
life, who enriched their profound devotion to the person
of Christ with a knowledge of the ancient ways such
as no "born Christian" can ever have.

Earlier references to the spread of communism in
Asia will have made it clear that the churches "under
three flags" have to fight today not on three fronts, but
on four, since communism presents itself, if not as a religion, as a power that can fill the gap left by the fading
away of a traditional religion. It is essential that Christian leaders, indeed all Christians who are likely to be
faced by Communist influences or converts, should
have a good understanding of theoretical communism and
of the points at which it challenges Christian faith. They
should be able to set forth, not the Christian answer to
communism, but the Christian answer to those questions that communism is so pertinently raising. Investiga-
tion has shown that little has as yet been done by the
churches to give the necessary training to their members
and that hardly any literature on the subject as yet
exists in any Indian language. Here is one of the chief
defects in the Christian armor today. Competent prepa-
ration to meet the Communist may be for the churches

---

[1] *I Follow After* (New York, Oxford University Press, 1951), the
autobiography of Lakshmibai, Tilak's wife, can be recommended
without qualification to the student. More than any other book I
have ever read, this artless narrative takes the reader by the hand
and leads him into the intimate life of a high caste Indian family.

an even more urgent task than the discovery of new methods of approach to the three ancient religions.[1]

Evangelism in the modern world must be total evangelism, the confrontation of one total view of reality, one comprehensive way of life, with another. It must present Christ both as the fulfillment of that which the other religions are sincerely seeking where it is not to be found and as the positive answer to the denials by which they stand.

The Hindu affirms that Ultimate Reality is unknowable; he must be shown that, though it is true that "no man hath seen God at any time," the Ultimate Reality is already known, since perfectly revealed in the Incarnation, Death, and Resurrection of Jesus Christ.

The Buddhist stands for man's confidence in himself. It must be brought home to him that man can have no such ultimate confidence and can find firm standing ground only in the acknowledgement of sinfulness and need and in the forgiveness that God has made available in Christ.

The Muslim, ceaselessly confronted with the contrast between Jesus as he really was and Mohammed as he really was, must be helped to see that the teaching of Jesus, so far from being a special ethic for superior persons, points the way by which very ordinary people can be transformed through grace into likeness to their Master.

The real task is in convincing the Hindu of the validity of the Christian claims about the Ultimately Real. Only then will he see the significance of "conversion" as against

[1] A special committee appointed by the National Christian Council is dealing with this problem, especially with the provision of simple literature in the Indian languages.

"proselytism," the incompatibility of "uniqueness" and "finality" with "tolerance" and "syncretism," and the cosmic purpose of evangelism as against the temporal good work of "missions." We ourselves ought to be clear in our minds as to the fundamentals of our faith. More than our proclamation of the gospel message, the effective thrust is in the demonstration of the Christian "outlook" as vividly contrasted with the Hindu "outlook"; in more than in mere words, however compelling, or even in deeds, however appealing, it is lives that tell.[1]

The quotations in this section from leaders in the younger churches may serve to underline the statement that the evangelization of the Indian subcontinent is still in its first beginnings. This gives its exciting character to the new period that is now opening before us. So far there are few signs that the Asian churches have realized the greatness of their vocation in the twentieth century. On their ability to realize it and to rise to the height of it depends, humanly speaking, the future of one fifth of the human race.

[1] Devanandan, *op. cit.*, p. 346. Used by permission.

5

Let Us Unite

TOWARD CLOSER FELLOWSHIP

At the end of the eighteenth century, only three Protestant missionary societies were at work in India, the Danish-Halle Lutheran mission in the far south, the English Baptist Missionary Society, with its headquarters in Bengal, and the London Missionary Society, also in the far south. No American missionary had as yet arrived in India. With the beginning of the nineteenth century and the gradual removal of the restrictions imposed by the East India Company, missionaries of many churches and countries began to arrive, until, as we have seen, the Christian map of India is almost as complicated as that of the United States.

To the early missionaries divisions among Christians did not present any serious difficulties. They were familiar with the existence of many churches in one area in their home countries, India was very large and there was room for all, and on the whole they managed to work together without friction. And for the non-Christians the difficulties were much less than is often supposed. Both Hinduism and Islam are religions of many sects, and the existence of sects among Christians caused little surprise, though it did present difficulties when a man was thinking of becoming a Christian.

This situation of a simple acceptance of the Western divisions of Christianity could not go forever unchallenged. In many areas overlapping caused obvious waste of effort when missionaries were few and the greater part of India was still unevangelized. Uncomfortable episodes could and did take place. One of the early high caste converts in Bengal had been brought to the knowledge of Christ by Alexander Duff, the great pioneer of educational missions, who was a Scottish Presbyterian. Dr. Duff could not but be a little hurt and perplexed when the young man sought baptism from the English chaplain in Calcutta and joined the Anglican Church. Almost in spite of themselves, missionaries were driven to ask whether there was not some better way of organizing their work.

The first method of seeking closer fellowship was that of conference. From 1854 on, a great series of missionary conferences was held, attended by representatives of almost all the missions (always, of course, with the exception of the Roman Catholics). All the problems of missionary work were discussed with the greatest freedom, and underneath the denominational differences a wide range of agreement and fellowship was discovered.

As a result of the great World Missionary Conference at Edinburgh in 1910, steps were taken to give this fellowship a permanent organ and means of expression in India, and the National Missionary Council came into being. In 1923, this was transformed into the National

Christian Council. It was laid down that half the membership must be Indian. From the date of its foundation, the council has grown in strength and influence, has gained the confidence of the great majority of the Protestant missions, has guided them toward unity in thought and action without seeking to impose rules or policies on them, and is recognized by the government as its regular point of contact with Protestant missionary effort.[1]

The second step in cooperation was the adoption of rules of comity. Missions agreed not to open up work in areas where another mission was already established and not to work along lines of competition and rivalry. Where possible, the responsibility of missions and churches for certain areas was recognized, and their boundaries were respected by others. Thus in the south, the district of Madurai became almost wholly American Congregationalist, South Arcot Danish Lutheran, North Arcot American Dutch Reformed, Malabar Swiss and German Basel Mission. The very absurdity of these titles on the plains of India indicates the nature of the problems caused by the disunity of the church of Christ.[2]

The third step was direct cooperation in major enterprises. We have referred elsewhere to the medical col-

[1] Owing to the political developments, separate Christian Councils for Ceylon and West Pakistan have now come into being. Missionary societies which are not associated with the N.C.C. have direct access to the government.

[2] It is to be noted that, though almost all the larger missions agreed to regard themselves as bound by these rules, a considerable number of smaller bodies refused to accept them and felt themselves free to take up work wherever the Spirit moved them.

leges at Vellore and Ludhiana. These are only two of a great number of united enterprises. The Madras Christian College, originally an enterprise of the Church of Scotland, came to be supported by the Anglican and other missions. The Women's Christian College in Madras was founded as a union institution and is now maintained by twelve missionary societies in Britain, Canada, and the United States. The majority of theological students in India receive their training in union theological seminaries, such as Serampore College in Bengal, founded by the English Baptists, or the United Theological College of South India and Ceylon at Bangalore, founded as a joint enterprise in 1910 with its first principal a distinguished Danish Lutheran.

A fourth method was the development of denominational bodies on an all-India basis. Here the Anglicans were first in the field. In 1835 the Bishop of Calcutta was recognized by Act of Parliament as Metropolitan of the whole of India, and since that date all Anglican development in India has taken place within the framework of a single Anglican fellowship, served by several missionary societies. In 1930 the Anglican Church in India was separated from the Church of England and became the independent Church of India, Burma, and Ceylon, still within the world-wide fellowship of the Anglican Communion. In 1926 the Federation of Evangelical Lutheran Churches in India and Pakistan was formed; of the ten Lutheran Churches in the area, nine, with a membership of over half a million, belong to the federation. In general, Lutherans in India are more concerned with strengthening the federation than with the outreach to Christians of other denominations.

By various means, the non-Roman forces in India have been led to a considerable degree of fellowship and common action. But none of these methods separately nor all of them together have solved all the problems of Christian division.

The boundaries worked out under plans of comity are inevitably in some ways artificial. Two closely related families living on opposite sides of a river might decide to become Christians at the same time and might find themselves in separate churches, separate to the extent of having no mutual rights of admission to Holy Communion. Thus the converts might find that by the adventure of becoming Christians they had lost that unity which they had had as members of a single Hindu caste. Twenty years ago, the Ezhavar community in Travancore, nearly a million strong, became dissatisfied with the lack of social privilege to which its members were condemned in Hindu society and showed signs of moving in a mass toward Christianity. The discovery that as Christians they might be divided up among five or six rival churches brought the movement rapidly to an end.

Again, comity rules would work reasonably well if Christians would stay where they are. But Indian Christians are as mobile as other folk. They move from the country to the town and from one area to another for longer or shorter periods of work. Are the churches to which they belong to follow them into the new area or transfer them to some other denomiation? Anglicans and Lutherans, whose rules of communion are stricter than those of some other bodies, have tended to follow the faithful. The result is seen in small, isolated groups clinging to their own traditional forms of worship and church order, visited perhaps once in three or four months by a pastor who has to travel hundreds of miles to reach them, and remaining in total isolation from the other Christians within easier reach of them. But is not this the logical consequence of denominationalism? The issue has been put pungently by one of the greatest living authorities on Christian union:

Because the churches belong to different denominations, the cause of Christ is represented in one place by Episcopalians, in another by Presbyterians, in another by Baptists, and so on, each denomination having its own rules regarding church membership and church government. . . . What then is to be done? Two ways only are open. One is to work for the establishment in every center of the full range of denominational churches, so that any Christian, as he moves about the country, may find wherever he goes a congregation which abides by the ecclesiastical rules and practices in which he has been brought up. The other is to seek for reunion.[1]

Faced with this alternative, a number of the Protestant churches in India decided to try the way of organic union.

CHURCH UNION IN SOUTH INDIA

¶ One of the first great achievements was the formation, in 1908, of the South India United Church, a body that brought together most of the Presbyterians and Congregationalists in South India in a fellowship that was distinctly more than a federation but rather less than an organic union of churches as that is gen-

[1] *The Reunion of the Church*, by J. E. Lesslie Newbigin, pp. 20-21. New York, Harper and Brothers, 1948. Used by permission.

erally understood. During the first world war, the continental element was brought in, when the Malabar District of the Basel Mission, then temporarily under the care of British and American missionaries, entered the S.I.U.C.

The first step having been taken, matters could not rest there. Eleven years later a definite challenge was flung out to all the churches in India. A group of ministers, all but two of whom were Indians, had met at Tranquebar, the little port town at which the first non-Roman missionaries to India had landed in 1706, to consider the problems of division and unity. They found themselves led to affirm that one of the gravest obstacles to the evangelization of India is the divisions between the Christian churches. The Tranquebar declaration is recognized to have been the starting point of one of the greatest union movements in the history of the church.

We believe that the union is the will of God, even as our Lord prayed that we might be one, that the world might believe. . . . We believe that the challenge of the present hour . . . and the present critical situation in India itself call us to mourn our past divisions and turn to our Lord Jesus Christ to seek in him the unity of the body expressed in one visible church. We face together the titanic task of the winning of India for Christ—one fifth of the human race. Yet, confronted by such an overwhelming responsibility, we find ourselves rendered weak and relatively impotent by our unhappy divisions—divisions for which we were not responsible, and which have been, as it were, imposed upon us from without, divisions which we did not create and which we do not desire to perpetuate.[1]

[1] The Tranquebar Statement is to be found in full in *Documents on Christian Unity*, ed. by G. K. A. Bell, pp. 278-81. London, Oxford University Press, 1924.

It is important to note the order preserved in the statement. The signatories first affirmed that unity was the will of Christ; they then went on to point out that disunity was a grave practical hindrance to the work of the churches. In all the long negotiations that followed, this order was preserved. Practical and pragmatic needs were never allowed to obscure the fact that a true union of churches can come only through faith and through obedience to the will of God, as he is pleased to reveal it.

The two churches immediately concerned—the S.I. U.C. and the Anglican Church in India—quickly took action and set up committees to work together in search of such a union as would not involve the absorption of one church by another but would preserve the liberty of each to contribute to the whole the full riches of its own tradition. In 1925 the Methodist Church also joined in the negotiations.[1] Thus began a period of effort that after the lapse of almost the full span of a generation of human life resulted in the formation of the Church of South India on September 27, 1947.

From the start there were many factors favorable to union. Many of the leaders in the three churches knew one another intimately from long cooperation in common tasks. All the churches had learned much from one another. The Anglicans had developed a complete system of councils, democratically elected, through which the lay people were accustomed to take a full share in

[1] This refers to the church that was the fruit of the labors of the British Methodists. The Methodist Church in Southern Asia, linked to the Methodist Church in the United States, did not take part in the negotiations.

the ordering of the church's life. The nonepiscopal churches had found it necessary, under the conditions of the mission field, to develop a form of pastoral superintendence that fulfilled many of the functions of episcopacy, without the name, and in some cases gave to chairmen or superintendents more power than is ordinarily exercised by an Anglican bishop.

Yet there were many difficulties to be overcome. It was not easy to convince Congregationalists that any way could be found of reconciling the autonomy of the local congregation with diocesan organization and the authority of a bishop. The Anglicans insisted on the retention of the historic creeds; some other churches were unaccustomed to the use of creeds and instinctively distrusted them. All were prepared to agree that God had used and blessed the ministries of all the churches concerned; not all could be brought to agree as to the full equality and validity of all these ministries. Nor were these divisions confined to missionaries from the West. It is sometimes stated that, if Indians could be left alone to work things out for themselves, they would quickly liquidate the imported divisions and find the way to unity. Experience shows that this is not true. The missionaries have done their work too well; they have so indoctrinated their pupils that some among them cling with passionate devotion to every detail of the tradition as it has come to them from the West, and sometimes more eagerly to the details than to the central issues of the faith.

As recent studies have reminded us, the nontheological factors in division are often as influential as the strictly theological. People fear to lose in a union that which has been precious to them in separation. We are all attached to particular forms in worship, even to the tunes we use in singing our hymns. We find ourselves ill at ease in worship of a different tradition. Indian Christians felt strong ties of loyalty to the churches in the West from which the gospel had been brought to them and had no wish to relax those ties in favor of a local union. All kinds of fears, prejudices, and apprehensions had to be slowly and patiently worn down before union became psychologically possible.

But through twenty-eight years the work of discussion went steadily on, and gradually the lineaments of a united church began to appear. Certain basic principles were laid down, from which the churches never afterwards departed.

On questions of faith no great difficulties were encountered. All the churches were agreed as to the supremacy of Scripture; all were ready to accept the Nicene Creed as the authorized summary of the faith. No attempt was made to work out in advance an elaborate confession of faith or to reach agreement on every detail. Some critics of the scheme have been surprised that churches could agree to come together on so brief and general a profession of the faith. But those who made the Church of South India were convinced that it was necessary to believe that the Holy Spirit would continue to work after the union had been formed and that there were many questions of detail that could be settled only through the experience of common life in a united church.

At an early date it was decided that there should be no question of reordination or recommissioning of any ministers in any of the uniting churches. All agreed to accept the historic episcopate as one element in the life of the united church and to commit to the bishops, with the assistance of other ministers, the responsibility for all ordinations after union. But all the ministers of the uniting churches were to be accepted on an equal basis, with the safeguard that no congregation should have forced on it a ministry that it could not conscientiously accept. This would mean that at the start there would be some ministers who had been ordained by bishops and others who had not. Such an arrangement would be highly irregular from the Anglican point of view, and this irregularity would persist until in course of time the whole ministry of the united church was unified under a single form of ordination. But this seemed the only honest way to deal with a situation that would not yield to more radical and sudden treatment. When divisions have persisted for centuries, is it much to ask that a period of thirty years or so should be allowed for growing together, before the union can be regarded as in every way complete?

At last the time came when the churches had to ask themselves, not whether unity was in itself desirable, but whether in view of the unity already achieved they had any right longer to remain in separation. To this it seemed that there could be only one answer. Some questions still remained to be answered. There were strong criticisms of the scheme both from the Anglican and from the Free Church side. There were as yet unrelieved anxieties, lest the loss involved in union might be greater than the gain. But, when agreement had been reached on the essentials of the faith and on so much in the order and organization of the church, it seemed that to refuse to go forward into unity might involve direct disobedience to the will of God. During 1944 and 1945 all the church bodies concerned voted in favor of the scheme and of the consummation of union. September 27, 1947, was fixed as the day on which the scheme should come into effect.

On the appointed day, in the Cathedral of St. George at Madras, the inauguration of the new church took place. It was solemnly declared that the uniting churches were no longer three but one, one church with more than a million baptized members. Then nine new bishops were consecrated to share with the five Anglican bishops already in office the care of the fourteen dioceses into which the area of the church had been divided. Of the nine, some were Indians, some were Europeans (as it happens, no American, but there is no reason why in future elections an American Congregationalist or Presbyterian should not be chosen), some were Anglicans, others drawn from the Free Churches. Thirty-five hundred Christians joined in the service of Holy Communion with which the inaugural service concluded. To all who were present on the auspicious occasion it was a day of great joy.

Other unions of churches have been larger, but none has ever had greater significance in the life of the Christian church as a whole. For the first time in the four centuries since the Reformation, the gap between the episcopal and nonepiscopal churches has been bridged. Episcopalians have gladly accepted the treasures that God has given to his church through the nonepiscopal traditions; nonepiscopalians have freely accepted episcopacy as a gift of great value, through which the unity of the church can be maintained and expressed.

The union was not achieved without creating fresh division. In the Nandyal area of the Telugu country, 30,000 Anglicans refused to enter the union, and maintained their former Anglican position. This division has led to painful and bitter disputes, and, though the situation has gradually improved, it is unlikely that unity in this area will soon be achieved.

The new church has been vigorously criticized in many quarters, especially by high Anglicans, who regard it, especially in the matter of its mixed ministry, as a betrayal of the principles of church order that they hold dear. The Lambeth Conference of Anglican bishops in 1948, while giving thanks for the measure of unity locally achieved by the inauguration of the Church of South India, pledging itself to pray and work for its development into an ever more perfect fulfillment of the will of God for his church, and looking forward hopefully and with longing to the day when there shall be full communion between the Church of South India and the Anglican Communion, did not feel it possible to accord more than limited recognition to the new church.[1]

It was recognized by those who entered into the union that the process of growing together would take a long time and could not be hurried. But the church has held together, and after several years can look back on certain solid achievements.

The new church was constituted in the hope that it would be able to move forward into an ever enlarging

[1] *Lambeth Conference, 1948.* Part I, pp. 37-40; Part II, pp. 41-9.

union. Within a very short time after the inauguration, it opened up discussions with the Lutherans and the Baptists. These, though friendly, have not yet led to any practical results.

While leaving to the churches freedom in the use of the forms of service to which they were previously accustomed, the C.S.I. has set to work to develop its own forms of worship. Its order for the Holy Communion has been highly approved by liturgical scholars in many countries and is finding increasing acceptance in the church. Experimental forms for confirmation and baptism are in use, though due to be revised before they are finally adopted.

In dioceses such as South Travancore or Tinnevelly, where almost all the Christians belong to one tradition, the union has not made much difference. In dioceses where many missions have previously been at work, much progress has been made in the complicated process of unifying all their organizations and particularly their finances.

But the greatest gain of all is in a region where it is difficult to find exact expression for what has happened. The aim of the union was that all the uniting traditions should be preserved and that none should be submerged by the others. All the leaders in the church say that now they have the feeling that they are the heirs of all the previously separated traditions. They are less and less conscious of what they were before the union—Anglicans, Methodists, or Presbyterians—and more and more conscious of belonging to a fellowship that is greater than any of its separate parts.

Sometimes onlookers see more of the game. Visitors

to the Church of South India have been remarkably unanimous in their affirmation that, though the union is still incomplete, what has come into existence is a church, rejoicing in a spiritual sense of unity, and not just an amalgam of separate units. For instance, the bishop of Chichester, Dr. George Bell, who is also chairman of the Central Committee of the World Council of Churches, felt able to write after personal observation:

I [was] immensely impressed by the freshness and spontaneity, as well as the wisdom, of the leadership in its many aspects, and by the mingled modesty and confidence with which all whom we saw tackled their tasks. It is not easy to say which of two conspicuous characteristics struck us more forcibly; the reality of the *church* or the added power of *evangelization* afforded by the union. Indeed the two go together. Here is no association of constituent churches, but one church. And surely the coming together of even one million non-Roman Christians in South India . . . is a significant evangelistic achievement.[1]

Church union does not of itself bring spiritual renewal or a fresh evangelistic passion. In fact, it may have at first the opposite effect, since the elimination of the motive of rivalry or competition may lead to a lowering of the temperature and a weakening of effort. Yet looking back over the first five years of the life of the church, the moderator, A. M. Hollis, bishop of Madras, was able to express himself in terms of moderate hopefulness:

I can do little more than give my own impression that there is a real movement of self-questioning, a real seeking

[1] *The Ecumenical Review*, Vol. II, no. 3, pp. 250-1. Used by permission.

after something more than a conventional religion, a seeking to bear witness in many places. This has been helped by the contact of tradition with tradition, the richer resources now at our disposal, and more joint efforts within our new fellowship. Much remains to be done. Yet I believe it is true to say that more people than before are realizing that the only adequate foundation is Jesus Christ. There is not much to be said in India today for being a Christian unless one is going to be a real Christian.

More impressive even than the achievements of the Church of South India in its own area is the effect that it has had on the movement for church union throughout the world. Many plans for union, in parts of the world as far separated as Great Britain, Iran, and Nigeria, bear the South India impress deeply upon them, some of them repeating page after page of the South India Scheme of Church Union almost without a change. Naturally the influence was strongest in the areas most closely contiguous to South India, Ceylon and North India.

OTHER PLANS FOR UNION

¶ We may remind the reader that it is a great mistake to imagine that, because Ceylon is near to India, it is a part of it. Ceylon is very conscious of having a history, a civilization, and a spirit of its own. In church affairs, the Anglican diocese of Colombo is a part of the Church of India, Pakistan, Burma, and Ceylon, but did not enter the Church of South India. The mission of the American Board (Congregational Christian) in the North of Ceylon was part of the old South India United Church and did therefore enter the Church of South India as the diocese of Jaffna.[1] But it was evident from the start that, if Ceylon as a whole was to have a united church, it must work in its own way and produce its own independent scheme. The first step toward union was taken in 1934. In 1941 an official committee, representing all the churches that were members of the National Christian Council of Ceylon, began its work.

Ceylon had to face one problem that was not encountered in South India. In South India none of the Baptist bodies entered into the negotiations; in Ceylon British Baptists did. Is it possible, to use the traditional phrases, to combine the Paedo-Baptist and the Antipaedo-Baptist positions in the same church? It has never been done in history, but the twentieth century is the century of new experiments, and churchmen in Ceylon decided that it should be tried. Provision is made both for the baptism and for the dedication of children, for baptism of infants and for baptism of believers, and for the confirmation of all, at whatever stage of life they have previously been baptized.

One of the features of the Church of South India that has been most criticized is the continuance within it, over a long period of unification, of two types of ministry, the episcopal and the nonepiscopal. The negotiators in Ceylon decided, if possible, to eliminate this difficulty. Would it be possible to find a form of recommissioning, which, without being a reordination or throwing doubt on the ordination that ministers had

---

[1] Bishop Sabapathy Kulandran, the first bishop of Jaffna, is well known in America, personally and through his book *The Message and the Silence of the American Pulpit*. (Boston, Pilgrim Press, 1949.)

already received, would convey a new and wider authority to minister in the United Church of Lanka (Ceylon)? The Scheme of Union for Ceylon contains such a form of recommissioning. The new church, if it comes into being, is to be episcopal. After the inauguration, the bishops are to receive any ministers who desire it, with prayer and the laying on of hands, into the wider fellowship of the ministry of the united church. It is hoped that such a commissioning for wider service will make the ministers who have received it acceptable as ministers throughout the whole of the united church, and will avoid such difficulties in relation to churches outside Ceylon as South India has experienced.

The Scheme of Union has naturally met with a good deal of opposition, as such schemes always will. One small church has withdrawn from the negotiations. One group of Anglicans is vociferous in its criticisms. But in general the scheme has roused much interest and has been well received, the Lambeth Conference of Anglican bishops (1948) commending it as "of singular interest and promise." Some years must pass before the churches concerned can pass any final decisions on the scheme.

North India did not remain unaffected by the general interest in questions of church union. The first meetings of the still continuing series were held in 1929 and 1930. At long last an almost complete Scheme of Union for North Indian Christians was proposed in 1951.

In North India, as in South, the negotiators were able to start from a measure of union already achieved. Here it was the Presbyterians who had taken the initiative and had the finest record of achievement. Presbyterian missions had their origin in all the four countries of the British Isles, as well as in Canada, the United States, and New Zealand. All these missions held the same doctrine and polity, and there was nothing to keep them separate except the accident of geographical origin. Even before the end of the nineteenth century, most of the Presbyterian groups had been brought together in the Presbyterian Alliance in India. More important, in view of present developments, was the step taken in 1904, when almost all the Presbyterian groups came together in a single Presbyterian Church, which, while not uniting the organizations of the different missions, made available to Indian Christians a much wider fellowship than they had enjoyed before, one rooted in the soil of India and not in Western lands. It was on the basis of this experience that further steps toward union could be taken.

In 1924 the United Church of Northern India came into being and unified the work of ten missionary societies, American and British, mostly Presbyterian and Congregational. The six synods and twenty-five councils of this church extend over an enormous area from the northeastern hills on the borders of Assam to the western sea at Bombay, and from the heights of the Himalayas to the heart of the dry and burning Deccan. With this far-flung church are associated in the continuing negotiations the Anglican Church, the Baptists, the British Methodists, and the Methodist Church in Southern Asia, the representative in India of the great Methodist Church of the United States.

North India has learned a great deal from South and in some respects has followed Ceylon. Since the Baptists are in on the negotiations, there is the same provision as in Ceylon for both baptism of infants and baptism of believers. There is a similar attempt to unify all the ministries from the moment of union.

But the course of church union negotiations has never run smooth, and North India has struck a new difficulty. Within the churches that are seeking union, there are already two forms of episcopacy, the Anglican, which claims historic and unbroken connection with the church of the days of the apostles, and the Methodist, which makes no such claim to succession but looks back to the great outpouring of the Spirit of God in the work of the Wesleys. For a long time it proved impossible to find a way by which these two traditions of episcopacy could be reconciled and combined in one church, and the negotiations almost broke down on this point. It was only toward the end of 1953 that the committee was able to announce that it had found an acceptable solution for this problem, and to forward a completed Scheme of Union to the churches for their consideration and decision.

The latest development is the proposal for a united church in West Pakistan. The relationships between India and Pakistan are such as to cause constant difficulty and anxiety to churches and missions that have work on both sides of the frontier. It has already been found desirable to create a Christian Council of West Pakistan in separation from the Christian Council of India. This council at its first meeting invited the five churches of which it is made up to join in appointing a Church Union Committee, to work on the scheme proposed for North India, to introduce into it such modifications as might seem desirable in view of conditions in Pakistan and so to prepare the way for a united church in Pakistan. In addition to the Anglicans, Methodists, and the United Church (itself the result of union between a wide range of missions and churches), the five churches concerned include the United Presbyterians and the Associated Reformed Presbyterian Church. Negotiations have as yet hardly begun, and it is not possible to say what success will come out of them in the future.

In considering such negotiations, it is well neither to be too optimistic as to progress nor to be too much depressed by checks which may be no more than temporary. In view of the strength of the desire for closer union among Christians in Asia and the vitality and stability manifested by the Church of South India, it is possible to hope that all these negotiations may end in success sometime within the next ten years. If this were achieved, the Christian map of the Indian subcontinent would show, instead of the present divisions, four great churches, resembling one another in general pattern, but each with its special characteristics, all in communion and closest fellowship with one another. These churches would include about half the six million non-Roman Christians in the subcontinent. The ancient Syrian Churches would still be outside. The Lutherans, large sections of the Baptists, and most of the smaller missions would probably remain in separation and independence. But such a movement for union steadily grows and attracts others, and it may well be that before the end of the ten years' period we have indicated, many other groups will find themselves drawn into a fellowship to which as yet they have not found it possible to give their adherence.

At the Madras Missionary Conference of 1938, the representatives of the younger churches gave poignant expression to their sense of the need for union and appealed earnestly to leaders in the home churches and in the mission boards not to stand in the way of union, which in the West might seem a luxury, but which in the East is a matter of extreme urgency:

> Loyalty . . . will forbid the younger churches going forward to consummate any union unless it receives the whole-hearted support and blessing of those through whom these churches have been planted. We are thus often torn between loyalty to our mother churches and loyalty to our ideal of union. We, therefore, appeal with all the fervor we possess to the missionary societies and boards and the responsible authorities of the older churches to take this matter seriously to heart, to labor with the churches in the mission field to achieve this union, to support and encourage us in all our efforts to put an end to the scandalous effects of our divisions, and to lead us in the path of union—the union for which our Lord prayed, through which the world would indeed believe in the Divine Mission of the Son, our Lord Jesus Christ.[1]

Ecumenical sense is highly developed in the Indian churches. Their desire is both to be free to be themselves and at the same time to stand firmly within the unity of the whole church of Christ, to which it is their desire to make their own special and characteristic contribution. But the older churches tend to move slowly, weighed down as they are by the traditions of centuries, and there is a danger that they may frustrate by their

[1] *The Life of the Church*, Vol. 4 of *The Madras Series*, pp. 377-78.

immobility churches that see new opportunities and are eager to move forward more rapidly into union.

United churches would in no way wish to separate themselves from the West. Yet there is no doubt that, united, they would feel themselves more deeply rooted in the lands to which they belong and freer to develop in relation to the needs of those lands and their ancient civilizations. It is unlikely that an Indian church would remain tied to Western patterns of life and expression. But this can be regarded only as an advantage by those who believe that the existence of peoples, nations, and languages is part of the plan of God for his world and that the fullness of the church can be seen only when all peoples, nations, and languages bring their peculiar treasures into the City of God.

6

Why Missionaries?

CHRISTIAN LEADERSHIP

During the twentieth century the Indian churches have about quadrupled their numbers. Geographically they have steadily extended their range, penetrating into many regions that fifty years ago were entirely untouched by the gospel. Educationally they have risen high above the general average of the country, and in consequence have begun to play an increasingly effective part in its public life. But more remarkable than all these other changes put together has been the way in which in these fifty years these churches have developed from foreign colonies of Western churches into genuinely Asian churches, rooted in the soil and under indigenous leadership.

At the start it was inevitable that leadership should be entirely in the hands of the missionary. He who alone had a deep knowledge of the Scriptures and of Christian tradition was the teacher, the spokesman, and the guide. Especially where the church was growing rapidly among the backward classes, he might be the only educated man. It fell to him to represent the church in all its dealings with the government. He found himself the object of affectionate and often much too detailed imitation on the part of his flock. Even if at an early stage he tried to throw back on them responsibility for decisions as to the life and conduct of the believers, again and again he found it necessary to intervene to correct or suspend a decision made through a mistaken understanding of the meaning of the Bible. (A case is on record where it had to be explained to simple Christians that the rules about clean and unclean beasts to be found in the book of *Leviticus* were not binding on the faithful and that they need not as Christians deprive themselves of a number of articles of diet to which they were accustomed.)

Worst of all, the missionary was the paymaster. Ideas of self-support grew slowly, especially among the very poor. The Indian minister, the teacher, the evangelist, the Biblewoman were all servants of the mission, and their scanty pay came to them through the man who added the office of treasurer to all the other labors that he carried out for the good of the church. For a generation or two no one found this strange or thought that any other system was possible.

Today the cause of Indian leadership has already been won. Missionaries have always in theory held the view that the time would come when they would no longer be needed and the Indian church would stand entirely on its own feet. But in many areas this happy day was thought of as being still in a very distant future, and there is no doubt that missionaries put far too little trust in the capacity of their Indian friends and held on to power much too long. The result was that a number of the ablest Indian Christians were lost to the service of churches in which they could find no adequate scope for their gifts and that among those who remained there was some resentment, accentuated by the rising tide of national feeling and suspicion of the foreigner. The victory of Indian leadership has not been won without dust and heat. That it has been won becomes evident through the most cursory survey of the present state of the churches.

The Anglican Church in India has had since 1950 an Indian head, the Most Reverend Arabindo Nath Mukerjee, formerly bishop of Delhi, now bishop of Calcutta and metropolitan of the Church of India, Pakistan, Burma, and Ceylon. The deputy moderator of the Church of South India is the bishop of Rayalaseema, the Right Reverend H. Sumitra, a former Congregationalist. The Methodist Church in Southern Asia has as its bishop for the Bombay area John Subhan, a convert from Islam. One of the best known of Indian Christians is the Very Reverend Augustine Ralla Ram, for many years general secretary of the Student Christian Movement of India, Burma, and Ceylon, and a former moderator of the United Church of Northern India. Karachi, the capital of Pakistan, will have as its first Anglican bishop the Reverend Chandu Ray, well known for his work in connection with the Punjabi and Sindhi translations of the Bible. We have already noted that the director of the great medical college at Vellore is an Indian woman doctor, and the famous theological college at Serampore now has its first Indian principal, Dr. C. E. Abraham. Bangalore will have its first Indian principal, Russell Chandran, in 1954. Both the president, Mr. B. L.

Rallia Ram,[1] and the general secretary, Dr. E. C. Bhatty, of the National Christian Council of India are Indians, while one of the vice-presidents is a British bishop of the Church of South India, F. Whittaker of Medak. It would be tedious to extend what could easily become an endless list. The process of handing over responsibility to Indian leadership at the higher levels is far from complete, and some Indians feel that it is going forward much too slowly; nevertheless the progress recorded in a generation is remarkable and encouraging.

ARE MISSIONARIES STILL NEEDED?

¶ If all this has been done, are missionaries still needed, and if so, why? The answer to this question can only be given by Indian, Pakistani, and Ceylonese leaders themselves, and we may stop for a moment to consider the circumstances by which in part their answers are affected.

The history of recent development can be summed up in three words, submission, conflict, partnership. In some churches these three stages can be seen contemporaneously in operation.

On the whole the older men were prepared to accept without resentment the leadership of the missionary. Missionaries have made many mistakes, but they have a wonderful record of loving and devoted service to their people. The simple village pastor or teacher had no desire to enter into rivalry with his foreign friend. He had his own position and his own dignity. He might be a junior partner, but he felt himself to be emphatically

[1] To the sorrow of all his many friends, the death of Mr. Rallia Ram was announced when this chapter was already in manuscript.

a partner in a joint enterprise, respected both by the missionary and by the people among whom he worked.

A younger generation, that from which the greater part of the present leadership of the churches is drawn, was no longer prepared to acquiesce in this patriarchal arrangement. There was a new consciousness of worth and a desire for independence that had to find expression in a reconstruction of relationships. This was not achieved without bitterness. Sometimes there was a justified feeling of resentment against foreigners who desired to retain a control that was no longer needed or desired. Sometimes there was an admixture of less Christian motives of personal ambition and desire for power. The missionary found himself exposed to a ceaseless stream of cruel and often baseless criticism, his least word and action liable to be fantastically misinterpreted. Much equanimity was required to go on quietly in humble Christian service under such conditions.

The man of a still younger generation looks back on that painful period with undisguised astonishment. Accustomed to welcome the young missionary as a friend and colleague, to address him by his first name, to criticize him frankly to his face and to expect frank criticism in return, he wonders what all the pother was about and why such bitterness was felt and expressed by his elders. As the young people of this generation assume positions of leadership in the churches, it becomes evident that a further reconstruction of relationships is on the way. It is in Ceylon that this adjustment seems already to be nearly complete, and Ceylonese churchmen visiting India feel that the unresolved tension between missionaries and Indian leaders, which in some places continues to perplex the church and to weaken its witness, is one mark of the continuing adolescence of the Indian church.

When this tension is finally released, it will be possible to pose again, in a manner from which heat and emotion are excluded, the question of whether missionaries are still needed and, if so, why?

If the question is taken to mean, "Could the Indian churches survive if, as has happened in China, all foreign personnel was suddenly withdrawn?" the answer is emphatically, "Yes." In some backward areas, the work might collapse; in others it might be seriously weakened. In almost all, the Indian churches would be genuinely sorry to see their foreign friends depart. But the strength of local leadership is now such that they would carry on with little serious dislocation. But if the question means, "Can the Indian churches, as they now are, undertake without help and within any reasonable span of time, the total evangelization of their countries?" the answer must be quite different. When the younger generation is asked, "What do you want missionaries for?" the answer is unhesitating: "To help us finish the unfinished task."

The modern missionary movement developed under the inspiration of the slogan "The Evangelization of the World in this Generation." The leaders of those days made a distinction between evangelization, the clear preaching of the gospel, and conversion. They were not actuated by any false optimism that supposed that the whole world could be made Christian in thirty or fifty years. They held the view that the main purpose for which the church exists is to preach the gospel and that it is the business of each Christian generation to see that in its time, as far as possible, the gospel is preached throughout the world, no less to the new generation that is appearing in America at the rate of about three million babies a year than to the millions in China and Peru. About forty years ago the famous slogan was given up, and since then the Protestant missionary enterprise has been trying, without much success, to explain itself to itself and to the world. Emphasis has been laid on the planting and development of the church, a necessary emphasis; but now that the church has been planted and so far developed in almost every land, it is possible to ask again, "What is the church for?" The younger generation in southern Asia replies "To preach the gospel to every creature; and since we cannot do it all without your help, come over and help us."

If we press our inquiry further and ask, "In what parts of the church's work do you want help?", the answer will certainly be, "In every part. There is no part of the life of the church in which we are not producing our own experts and leaders, but they are far too few, and everywhere we still want your help."

This is interesting as a reaction against a policy that has been widely followed for a good many years. In many areas a separation had been made between "the church" and "the mission." The work of the local churches, pastoral and evangelistic, was handed over to "the church"; institutions, especially such higher institutions as the arts colleges and theological seminaries, were retained as the field of "the mission," and there was a general assumption that this would be the sphere of the missionary. His task would be to provide expert assistance in the posts for which there was no available

Indian and to give his time to the training of Indian leaders. This separation has not been of advantage to the development of the church. Since the institutions were not under the church, the churches in many cases felt no great responsibility for them. Those working in institutions, whether Indian or foreign, have tended to live in almost complete isolation from the life of the ordinary workaday church, sometimes regarding themselves as a class of superior beings, marked out by receiving from Western sources a far higher salary than the Indian churches would ever be able to pay.

Of late years the harm done by this separation has come to be vividly realized. In many areas the division between church and mission has been done away with, and the two have learned to come together facing jointly the total Christian task. This has led to the realization that, even in what was considered the area of "the church," the foreigner might still have many good gifts to give. In general it is true that the Indian makes the best evangelist among Indians. On the other hand, one of the most remarkable evangelistic efforts in the whole of India is the leaflet evangelism developed in Vellore under the direction of the scholar John H. Piet of the American Arcot mission. Piet was wholly absorbed in institutional work until his challenge to an Indian layman, "Why doesn't the church do something about evangelism?" was met by the counter challenge, "Why don't you do something about it?" [1] Very few foreigners

---

[1] "Leaflet and Newspaper Evangelism in South India," by John H. Piet in *World Dominion*, Sept.-Oct., 1951, pp. 271 ff. Used by permission.

Dr. Piet's extremely learned work on the Saiva Siddhanta philosophy can be recommended only to those who are prepared for some real tough going.

know an Indian language well enough to lecture in it acceptably to an educated non-Christian audience. But English is still the common language of educated India, and just as the American preacher is readily acceptable in Britain because the difference of accent and presentation lends freshness to what he says, the missionary in the East may still find a wide open door for the presentation of the gospel in English to the intelligentsia.[1] It is not a good thing that a foreigner should be the permanent pastor of a parish. But it would be good for every young ordained missionary to undergo a period of pastoral training under an experienced Indian pastor. He would find that from the riches of the Western pastoral tradition he would have certain things to give, as well as many lessons to learn.

LEADERSHIP FOREIGN AND INDIGENOUS

¶ It is taken for granted today that the missionary from the West must go out to put himself at the disposal of the church and joyfully serve under Asian leadership. But if we were to put to our younger Asian leader the question, "Does missionary service today afford scope for leadership as well as for service?", the immediate

---

[1] Apart from the great work of Dr. E. Stanley Jones, I may refer to a most interesting report by Mr. F. P. D. Penning of the Christian Literature Society. Mr. Penning had gone to a certain town to lecture to Christians on Christian literature. He was horrified to find himself faced by the whole of the local intelligentsia, Hindu, Muslim, and Christian, expecting a lecture on "The Place of Literature in the Modern World." "I have rarely had a more stimulating and appreciative audience, and I was told afterwards that 'our townsfolk love a lecture and rarely get the chance of hearing a new European.'" (*National Christian Council Review*, Oct., 1952, p. 448.) Used by permission.

answer would be, "We would no longer make the false distinction between leadership and service. You must come prepared to serve in any position that we put you into. If that position is at the bottom, you must be content, and if it is at the top, you must not let any false modesty prevent you from responding to the call of the church."

For more than a generation, missions and churches have concentrated on the policy of training "leaders for the church." Today the churches are bitterly aware of the dangers of a policy that tended to lay stress on qualities of leadership without adequate emphasis on inner and spiritual fitness. In the old days missionaries aimed at producing men and women of God. They produced many such men and women and in the process a considerable number of outstanding leaders. A later generation, aiming at the production of leaders, has produced a few leaders and too few men and women of God. Here is an Indian Bishop's view of the distortion that may befall a policy of Indianization, admirable in itself, if the spiritual resources of those concerned are inadequate to the demands made upon them:

Another movement which has been growing in the country is that of devolving more and more posts of responsibility and authority upon the Indian church. . . . But notice the effect of this movement on the life of the church. . . . Posts of responsibility and authority have lured Indian Christian workers away from discharging their legitimate responsibilities. Their one ambition seems to be to rise to higher posts of authority. The teacher wants to be a pastor, a pastor wants to be a district minister, a district minister a circle chairman, a circle chairman a bishop. Considerations of ability, experience, and the call from God are entirely ignored. Canvassing, competition, rivalry, dissension, and litigation are the snares in which we are caught. While devolution of authority into Indian hands is a very desirable object, it has diverted the attention of church workers and church members from their proper duties and considerably weakened the church in the discharge of its primary task.[1]

The Indian layman is often more critical of leaders of his own race than of his missionary friends. This has sometimes been startlingly seen in elections in which laymen have taken part. Recently a bishop had to be elected for the diocese of Mysore in the Church of South India, to take the place of the first bishop, Indian leader G. Gurushanta, whose untimely death was a grievous loss to his diocese and to the whole church. On the first list there were fifteen names, about equally divided between Indians and foreigners. After one vote, only five names were left and not a single Indian name among them. A Young British Methodist, N. C. Sargant, was elected and has since carried out his episcopal duties to admiration.[2]

This lay attitude came out clearly in a discussion in the Synod of the Church of South India in March, 1952. The European Moderator of the church initiated a discussion on the urgency of developing Indian leadership. His statement was discussed by three groups and a comment drawn up by each separately. The missionaries said that they had no wish to hold on to authority and were ready to move out whenever the church desired that they should do so. The Indian clergy said that:

[1] Bishop H. Sumitra of Rayalaseema in the *National Christian Council Review*, Oct., 1952, p. 431. Used by permission.

[2] Happily, in April, 1953, the diocese of Tinnevelly elected as its first Indian bishop the Reverend Augustine Jebaraj, B.A., B.D.

Where such positions of responsibility, now occupied by missionaries, can be immediately filled by competent Indians, men or women, measures should be taken to effect the necessary changes without further delay because, in our opinion, once appointed, opportunity and experience would give the Indians the needed training.

The Indian laymen said:

While recognizing that Indians can be and are leaders in the C.S.I., we are satisfied with the progress that has been and is being made in the matter of Indianization in the various dioceses. We feel that any preference on the basis of nationality to the exclusion of merit and efficiency is not desirable.

Mr. Rajaiah D. Paul, the secretary of the synod, in a long statement, affirmed among other things:

I do not mind if, at the present time and for a considerable time, the majority of the bishops of the Church of South India and its other leaders are foreigners. If the choice for any responsible office is between a mediocre and unworthy Indian and a foreigner better qualified and spiritually better equipped for holding such responsibility, I shall unhesitatingly today, tomorrow, and forever choose the foreigner. . . . I refuse to act under a false sense of nationalism. Our experiences in the recent past of the artificial replacement of the foreigner by the Indian are too bitter to allow us to make the same mistake and take the same risk in the Indian church.[1]

The churches in India, Pakistan, and Ceylon have affirmed over and over again in recent years that they desire the continued cooperation of colleagues from the

[1] *The South India Churchman*, February, 1952, pp. 3-16, for these quotations and for a full account of the debate. It should be added that, while the Synod re-elected Mr. Paul as its Secretary, many of its members were in strong disagreement with his views as expressed above.

West. From these various affirmations it is possible to put together a synthetic picture of the kind of missionary whom they are prepared to welcome.

THE PLACE OF THE MISSIONARY

¶ It is necessary that he should have some kind of qualification that lifts him above the average of the Indian church at its present level. From the point of view of that church, a missionary may seem to be a rather expensive luxury. Therefore if he is to be accepted in genuine partnership, the church must be satisfied that his contribution is of real value to it. The range of the Christian enterprise, as we have earlier depicted it, is so wide that there is hardly any special qualification for which a place cannot be found in the service of the Indian churches.

Just this variety of opportunity makes it possible for Christians from the West to render great service to the younger churches. A beginning has been made, for instance, in the exchange of teachers in theological seminaries, and great developments in this method of mutual enrichment are to be looked forward to. Teams of Western and Eastern Christians have worked together in relief and rehabilitation. Expert commissions have brought gifts of spiritual renewal as well as a trained judgment on the particular problems that were their special concern. But the younger churches are growing firmer in their affirmation that what they want is missionaries who will make the land of their vocation their home and will stay long enough to become in every respect a part of the church in which they have come to minister.

The long term missionary must be prepared to identify himself as fully as possible with the life of the church and people whom he has come to serve, joyfully accepting the discipline of the church and regarding himself as a member or minister of it. It is not necessary to carry this identification to the point of adopting all the customs of the country or wearing Indian dress. Some missionaries have done so with advantage, but in general the people do not desire it. They like the missionary to know how to wear Indian dress naturally and readily and to enjoy doing so on suitable occasions. For him to wear it all the time seems to them a kind of affectation, especially when so many educated men in Asia are taking to Western ways of dress. Far more important than any externals is a good knowledge of the local language. This demand represents a return to older ideas. It is not so long ago that educated Indians were positively discouraging missionaries from learning a language, on the ground that they could never do it well and that all the people they would come into close contact with could speak English. Now, with the growth of national feeling and the greater importance attached to the Indian languages, it is felt to be essential that the missionary should be well equipped in this respect.[1]

He must come prepared for a simple standard of living. In old days when missionaries rarely went away

[1] The present Bishop of Lahore once reminded me that before he went to India, he asked me what in my opinion were the three most important qualifications for a missionary, apart from a living faith in Jesus Christ, and that I replied, "That is easy. The first is the language and the second is the language and the third is the language." I have seen no reason to change my opinion.

for holidays, when there were no electric fans nor refrigerators and little was known about tropical diseases, it seemed essential that the missionary should have a large and lofty house, a palace compared with those provided for his indigenous colleagues. Now with the spread of modern amenities even to the villages and with the aid of modern medical science, it is possible for the Westerner with reasonable care to live a simple life in the tropics and to keep good health over many years. Some missionaries have tried to live under completely Indian conditions. This has usually ended in disaster, and is not required. American friends of missions have sometimes been disturbed to learn that missionaries ordinarily employ a number of servants. They have not perhaps realized that in many cases the missionary wife has been almost as much a full time servant of the church as her husband, and that, where for instance every drop of water has to be drawn from a deep well by hand, such unpaid service is possible only if much of the mere mechanical work of running a house is taken off her hands.

Even with simplicity of living, the Western servant of the church can hardly come down to the level of salary on which his Indian colleague is able to live. This has been and continues to be a source of bitterness and controversy, and a completely Christian solution has not yet been reached. Many leaders of the younger churches recognize that the salary of a missionary must bear some relation to standards of life in his own country as well as to those of his adopted country. But in lands where, even more than in America, a man's position in society is determined by the salary he draws, it is not easy for colleagues of different races who are drawing different rates of pay for doing the same work to reach a perfectly harmonious relationship. Probably there is no logical solution to the problem. It would be greatly eased if all in the younger churches could realize that to the missionary his higher salary is not a privilege that he grasps, but a cross that he is compelled to carry for the sake of keeping fit for his work.

The missionary must be ready for the closest possible association with colleagues of the younger church and for adventurous experiment. One of the most promising features of the Asian scene at present is the development of the *ashram* movement. The word *ashram* is often rather loosely used, but it is a convenient term to cover all those experimental pieces of Christian service in which a group of people live together in close fellowship, under some kind of rule of life, with special emphasis on simplicity and much time devoted to the life of prayer. The Eastern character of such communities and their special emphases make them appear less foreign than most other forms of Christian enterprise. And in them Western and Eastern Christians seem to have found the road to a closer fellowship of spirit and co-operation than is common in the churches as a whole. It is interesting to note that many of the best known and most successful *ashrams* have come into existence through the cooperation of two friends, one Asian and one Western. There are the Christukula Ashram at Tiruppattur, founded by Dr. S. Jesudasan and Dr. E. Forrester-Paton for medical work in the villages; the Bethel Ashram in Travancore, where Sister Rachel Joseph and Miss E. J. Neve have brought into being a great center for work among women; and the Vidivelli Ashram [1] in Tinnevelly, where Miss Joy Solomon and Miss M. M. Frost, after many years of successful college teaching, have devoted themselves to a particularly poor and backward area. It may be that, in the future, the *ashram* will be the sphere in which the missionary can best make his contribution to the life of the church.

He must come prepared for much frustration, criticism, and even hostility from his fellow Christians. Unless he is fortunate enough to be located in one of the areas where tension between East and West is at an end, he is likely to find himself in an atmosphere in which his motives are suspected, his actions misrepresented, and his plans frustrated by those whom it is his only desire to serve. If he goes on quietly and humbly with his work, in the end he will live all this down, but it takes time and infinite patience. It is essential that the intending missionary should be warned that such suffering is likely to be his lot and should arm himself against it. Far too many missionaries have become disheartened and disgusted during their first term of service and have not returned after their first spell of leave at home.

He must, above all things, to use an old-fashioned term, be a soul-winner. The National Missionary Society of India recently published a somewhat scathing contrast between the missionary of old and his successor today.

No tribute is too high, no praise is too exaggerated that one could give to the evangelistic work which the early missionaries did in our country. We in India owe a debt which we could never repay to the Christian missions and

[1] The Ashram of the Morning Star.

for their work in our midst. . . . One is surprised at times to see some of the present missionaries! Expert photographers, producers of cinema films, keen mechanics, authorities on agriculture and industrial pursuits, experts in constructing buildings, able administrators, bookkeepers and financiers; but when it comes to doing the one job for which they are supposed to have come to the country, that is evangelism, they feel that that work could be better done by the Indians than themselves, and feel satisfied to relegate it to their Indian workers, most of whom are their assistants.[1]

THE ONE ESSENTIAL

¶ There is no suggestion in this passage that the technical qualifications referred to are not needed or that they have not their place in the Christian enterprise today. All that this passage is concerned to do is to give a somewhat sharp reminder to missionaries that, whatever their particular employment, they must be primarily concerned about the one essential thing; they must set themselves all the time and in every way to the winning of men and women for Christ, since in no other way can the church live and grow in a non-Christian country.

The missionary must be a man or woman of God, and recognizably so. The younger churches in India, Pakistan, and Ceylon are deeply and humbly conscious of their own spiritual poverty and their inadequacy to the task of winning one fifth of the human race for Christ. When a new missionary comes, they turn to him wistfully, saying, though not aloud, "Have not you, with your background of fifteen centuries of Christian faith, something that we have not as yet attained? Can

[1] *All India Council of the National Missionary Society of India,* Dec. 28, 1950-January 1, 1951, pp. 91-92.

you not set us an example of Christian discipline? Can you not teach us, by example more than by word, to enter more deeply into the secret of prayer? Can you not show us more than we already know of the power of the Holy Spirit?" If they turn away disappointed, they may welcome the missionary and love him, but they will feel that he has failed them at the central point of all, that he has shown himself weak at the very point where they longed that he should be strong.

What all this adds up to is that Eastern peoples do not quickly nor readily give their hearts or their confidence to the foreigner. Their trust is something that has to be earned and to be deserved. But the gift once given is never withdrawn; when they have taken you as one of their own, you belong and you belong forever.

Perhaps I may be allowed to record here an experience of my own, which though slightly comic is one of the most precious memories of my twenty years' service as a missionary. During the great missionary conference at Madras in 1938, as I was crossing one of the wide open spaces of the college where we met, an Indian friend called out to me, "Aren't you coming to the meeting of the Indian delegation?" I said that I had heard nothing about it, to which he replied, "It's just beginning. Come along," so we went together. In the first five minutes I realized with horror that I had strayed into a meeting arranged for the Indian members only of the Indian delegation, to give them the opportunity to tell Dr. Mott and Dr. Paton exactly how awful missionaries are. I was the only missionary present. I rose apologetically, and said that, as I had obviously come to the wrong place, I would withdraw. Whereupon the Indians present with one voice said, "You stay where you are. You are one of us." So, like the prophet Ezekiel, I sat where they sat.

THE END OF THE MATTER

¶ By the time that this book is in the hands of the reader, it will be thirty years since I took up missionary service in India. If I were today thirty years younger than I am, would I make the same decision that I made in 1924? If a young man or woman today on the threshold of a career asks my advice, can I honestly advise him to make the same decision? For me the answer cannot be in any doubt.

Many things have changed since 1924.

The Eastern and Western churches now meet on a footing of perfect spiritual equality. The West has already greatly profited by the spiritual gifts of the younger churches in Africa and the East. The old patronizing attitude is gone forever.

Six Indian churches are now member churches of the World Council of Churches and by this membership are linked in an especially close relationship of mutual loyalty and service with the many American churches that are members of the same great fellowship.

The political independence of the three countries has laid new and great responsibilities on their citizens and brought them face to face with all the problems of life in a revolutionary world. What contribution will Christians make to the life of their countries in these days of rapid change? We may never say, "Christianity is a useful antidote to communism; therefore, let us spread Christianity in India." The gospel stands by its own claims and by nothing else. But it is evident that the churches, if they are faithful to their vocation, have much to give that is urgently needed in the now fluid society in the midst of which they live. In politics, in economic regeneration, in social reconstruction, by integrity, by compassion, by self forgetful service, they have a contribution of incalculable value to make. Already Christians are exercising far greater influence than their small numbers would suggest.

The spiritual independence of the churches has made them conscious in a new way both of their dignity as living branches in the one body of Christ and also of their spiritual poverty in the face of the new tasks that he has laid upon them. There was a danger for a time that the churches might become so deeply occupied with their own affairs as to forget their wider responsibilities. Now it is evident that they are taking seriously the task of making Christ known throughout their countries. It is not surprising that they feel uncertain of their strength to carry out so vast an enterprise.

What will be the attitude of the West, overburdened as it already is with its own problems, to the newly emancipated East? Will it continue to go out toward it in friendly support and cooperation? Or will it withdraw in a new isolationism and leave the East to find its own salvation? When states and governments are devising new forms of cooperation and mutual help, will the churches stand back and leave such efforts wholly to the secular arm?

Between 1924 and 1954 many things have changed. But the command of Christ stands unchanged; his gospel must be preached to the ends of the earth and to every creature. Today his call and his command are reinforced by the voice of the young churches. They turn to their companions in the West and say frankly and clearly, "The task that God has given us is too great for our unaided strength. You have brought us thus far upon the way. This is not the time to let us down." They are right. The Western churches have set their hand to the plow in Asia. They have no right now to turn back.

Reading List

A WIDE range of literature is available in most libraries on the general history and description of the Indian subcontinent. Space permits here only a brief selection of recent, available, and reasonably priced titles. For a more extensive list, write for the Bibliography on India, Pakistan, and Ceylon, price 15 cents, to the Missionary Research Library, 3041 Broadway, New York 27, N. Y.

The views of the authors represented here are not necessarily in harmony with those of the author and publishers of *Under Three Flags*.

Leaders of adult study groups are directed to *Adult Guide on India, Pakistan, and Ceylon*, by Irene Jones. Published by Friendship Press, New York, price 50 cents, it is available through book stores and literature depositories.

CHRISTIANITY IN INDIA, PAKISTAN, AND CEYLON

Chand of India, by Irene Mason Harper. New York, Friendship Press, 1954. Cloth $2.00; paper $1.25. The story of an Indian village boy who is busy discovering his own country. A story book for juniors.

Change of Heart, by Harold A. Ehrensperger. New York, Friendship Press, 1954. Cloth $2.00; paper $1.25. The story of a young Indian's search for life and purpose amid the turmoil and tensions of modern India.

Face to Face with India, by Roland E. Wolseley. New York, Friendship Press, 1954. Cloth $2.50; paper $1.25. A distinguished journalist interviews a cross section of Indian society and brings the reader face to face with the people and their problems.

Fig Tree Village, by Grace W. McGavran. New York, Friendship Press, 1954. Cloth $2.00; paper $1.25. A story of Indian children and their festivals, for the primary age.

Jeep Tracks, by Helen L. Bailey. New York, Friendship Press, 1954. Paper $1.00. The personal record of an evangelist's experiences in ministering to the villages of Central India.

The Cross Is Lifted, by Chandran Devanesen. New York, Friendship Press, 1954. Cloth $1.50; paper $1.00. A collection of devotional poems and meditations.

The Hidden Treasure, by Jean Bothwell. New York, Friendship Press, 1954. Cloth $2.00; paper $1.25. A junior high book telling the story of a Hindu boy's flight from Lahore during the partition period.

THE LANDS AND THE PEOPLE

And Gazelles Leaping, by Sudhindra N. Ghose. New York, The Macmillan Co., 1949. $3.50. Autobiographical sketches of Indian life.

Ceylon, by Sydney D. Bailey. New York, Longmans, Green and Co., Inc., 1952. $1.80. A one volume history of Ceylon, emphasizing the evolution of a nation and the ideas that have influenced its growth.

Ceylon, Pearl of the East, by Harry Williams. New York, The Macmillan Co., 1951. $5.00. The "past tense" section of this book gives a history of Ceylon from a Ceylonese-centered point of view, even though it was written in England through the resources of the Ceylon Association in London. The "present tense" gives a realistic account of the life of the Ceylonese today, an account made vivid by well chosen photographs. A 36-page Guide Book that is appended as an epilogue to this volume serves as an admirable Baedeker.

Cradle of the Clouds, by Sudhindra N. Ghose. New York, The Macmillan Co., 1951. $3.50. A sequel to *And Gazelles Leaping*.

Hindu Woman, by Margaret Cormack. New York, Columbia University Teachers' College, 1953. $4.00. A study of the modern Hindu woman and her potentialities in the new India.

House of Earth, by Dorothy Clarke Wilson. Philadelphia, Westminster Press, 1952. $1.75. A novel of the partition period.

India in the New Era, by T. Walter Wallbank. Chicago, Scott Foresman and Co., 1951. Cloth $3.25; paper $2.40. Deals primarily with the background of independent India, treating India since partition only in the final section of the book.

Interview with India, by John F. Muehl. New York, The John Day Co., Inc., 1950. $3.50. A popular account of Indian life today.

My India, by Jim Corbett. New York, Oxford University Press, 1952. $3.00. An appreciation of the Indian masses.

The Autobiography of an Unknown Indian, by Nirad C. Chaudhuri. New York, The Macmillan Co., 1951. $6.00. Another glimpse into Indian life.

The Indian Way, by Ranjee Gurdarsing Shahani. New York, Philosophical Library, 1951. $3.75. An Indian woman's viewpoint on life in India.

The Land and the Well, by Hilda Wernher, with Huthi Singh. New York, The John Day Co., 1946. $3.00.

The Life of Mahatma Gandhi, by Louis Fischer. New York, Harper and Bros., 1950. $5.00. A brief life of the great Indian leader.

The Population of India and Pakistan, by Kingsley Davis. Princeton, Princeton University Press, 1951. $7.50. A penetrating study of population problems.

This Is India, Pakistan, and Ceylon, by Constance Hallock. New York, Friendship Press, 1954. 50 cents. Concise text and well selected photographs show the life of the people.

HISTORY

India, by Cyril H. Philips. New York, Longmans, Green and Co., 1950. $1.60. A brief guide to Indian history.

India, a Short Cultural History, by Hugh G. Rawlinson. New York, D. Appleton-Century Co., Inc., 1938. $7.50. An excellent introduction.

India, Pakistan, Ceylon, edited by William N. Brown. Ithaca, Cornell University Press, 1951. $3.00. Treats background and history of these three nations.

The Story of India, by Jean Bothwell. New York, Harcourt, Brace and Co., 1952. $3.00.

INDIA SINCE PARTITION

Independence and After, by Jawaharlal Nehru. New York, The John Day Co., 1950. $3.00. Reflects the transition from colonial status to independence.

India since Partition, by Andrew Mellor. New York, Frederick A. Praeger, Inc., 1951. $2.50. A history since 1947.

PAKISTAN SINCE PARTITION

Pakistan, the Heart of Asia, by Liaqat Ali Khan. Cambridge, Harvard University Press, 1950. $3.00. The author was the first prime minister of the new state.

The Making of Pakistan, by Richard Symonds. Hollywood-by-the-Sea, Transatlantic Arts, Inc., 1950. $3.00. The Pakistan idea is followed from early Muslim settlements to dominion status.

RELATIONS WITH THE WEST

Ambassador's Report, by Chester Bowles. New York, Harper and Bros., 1954. $4.00 The intimate record of America's most successful ambassador to India.

India and British Imperialism, by Gorham D. Sanderson. New York, Bookman Associates, 1951. $4.50. Well written historical analysis; contains excellent bibliography.

India and the Awakening East, by Eleanor Roosevelt. New York, Harper and Bros., 1953. $3.00

India and the United States, by Lawrence K. Rosinger. New York, The Macmillan Co., 1950. $2.75. An introduction to the relationship between India and the United States.

India, Pakistan and the West, by Percival Spear. New York, Oxford University Press, 1949. $2.00. A useful guide to the present situation, with special reference to relations with the West.

The United States and India and Pakistan, by William N. Brown. Cambridge, Harvard University Press, 1953. $4.50. A good introduction to the Indian subcontinent for American readers.

RELIGIONS OF INDIA AND PAKISTAN

Introducing Hinduism, by Malcolm Pitt. New York, Friendship Press, 1954. Paper 60 cents.

Introducing Islam, by J. Christy Wilson. New York, Friendship Press, 1950. Paper 60 cents.

Man's Religions, by John B. Noss. New York, The Macmillan Co., 1949. $4.50. An excellent textbook.

The Great Religions of the Modern World, edited by Edward J. Jurji. Princeton, Princeton University Press, 1946. $3.75. Articles by American scholars on the various religions.

The Religions of Mankind, by Edmund D. Soper. 3rd ed. rev. New York, Abingdon-Cokesbury Press, 1951. $3.50. A popular textbook.

The Scriptures of Mankind, by Charles S. Braden. New York, The Macmillan Co., 1952. $6.50. A good brief introduction to the scriptures of the various religions.

Two Religions, by John McKenzie. Boston, The Beacon Press, 1952. $2.00. A comparative study of some distinctive ideas and ideals in Hinduism and Christianity.

BIOGRAPHY

Azariah of Dornakal, by Carol Graham. Toronto, The Macmillan Co., 1946. $1.65. Life of an outstanding Christian leader.

Eagle Books. Paper, 20 cents each. The following titles from this series of exciting adventure stories about the lives of great Christians have been selected for the "India, Pakistan, and Ceylon" theme:

4. *The Man Who Disappeared* (Sadhu Sundar Singh), by J. Reason.

6. *Unarmed among Outlaws* (Theodore Pennell), by B. Underhill.

8. *Temperature 126!* (Henry Martyn), by Hugh F. Frame.

13. *Young Man—Sit Down!* (William Carey), by L. H. Dalton.

20. *Elizabeth Undaunted* (Elizabeth Newman), by B. Underhill.

63. *Dr. Ida* (Ida Scudder), by Sheila Smith.

I Follow After, by Lakshmibai Tilak. Translated by E. Josephine Inkster. New York, Oxford University Press, 1951. $2.50. The widow of the famous Christian poet relates the story of her life and conversion.

Sam Higginbottom, Farmer. New York, Charles Scribner's Sons, 1950. $3.00. Autobiography of a renowned agricultural missionary.

That All May Be One, by J. E. Lesslie Newbigin. New York, Association Press, 1952. $1.50. The American edition of Bishop Newbigin's *South India Diary*, an intimate view of daily ministry in the Church of South India.

The Yellow Robe, by Cyril J. Davey. London, Student Christian Movement Press, 1950. The story of a well known Indian Christian, Sadhu Sundar Singh.

Index

THE AUTHOR

THE RIGHT REVEREND STEPHEN NEILL, an Irish Anglican, was born in 1900, the son of medical missionaries to India. After five years of study at Trinity College, Cambridge, he followed in the footsteps of his parents by going as a missionary to South India, where he served for twenty years. Most of his time was spent in small, remote villages, as evangelist, pastor, and theological teacher, but he occasionally emerged to deliver courses of lectures, which have been published in book form. For ten years he was a member of the Joint Committee on Church Union in South India. In 1938 he was elected Bishop of Tinnevelly by an electoral body that was 96 per cent Indian and 4 per cent European.

In 1944 he returned to Cambridge as Chaplain of Trinity College and lecturer in theology. Since 1947 he has traveled to the Far East, Africa, Canada, the United States, and other areas on special missions and projects for the World Council of Churches and the International Missionary Council. He has established a world-wide reputation as an eloquent preacher with a direct, unrhetorical approach.

Bishop Neill has been associate general secretary of the World Council and at present is secretary of a committee of the International Missionary Council devoted to the production of literature for newly literate peoples. Two of his recent books are: *Christian Society* and *Fulfill Thy Ministry.*

THE FORMAT

TYPE: ELEVEN POINT LINOTYPE JANSON, LEADED TWO POINTS · COMPOSITION, PRINTING, AND BINDING: AMERICAN BOOK-STRATFORD PRESS, NEW YORK · JACKETS AND PAPER COVERS: TRIGGS COLOR PRINTING CORPORATION, NEW YORK · MAP: CARTOGRAPHY BY DE MOLA CORPORATION, NEW YORK, PRINTING BY SCREENLESS COLORTONE CORPORATION, BROOKLYN · TEXT PAPER: S. D. WARREN'S #66 ANTIQUE.

Typographic design by Margery W. Smith
Binding by Louise E. Jefferson

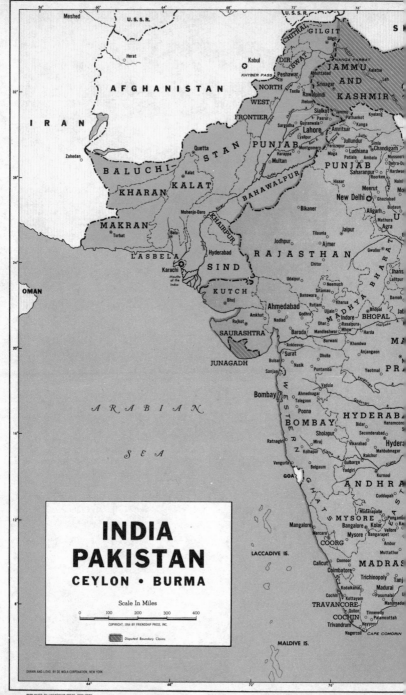

INDIA
PAKISTAN
CEYLON • BURMA

Scale In Miles

0   100   200   300   400

COPYRIGHT, 1954 BY FRIENDSHIP PRESS, INC.

Disputed Boundary Claims

DRAWN AND LITHO. BY DE MOLA CORPORATION, NEW YORK

PUBLISHED BY FRIENDSHIP PRESS, NEW YORK

Meshed

U.S.S.R.

U.S.S.R.

CHITRAL GILGIT S

Gilgit

Herat

Kabul

DIR

SWAT NANGA PARBAT

Kalatse

Leh

KHYBER PASS Peshawar

JAMMU

Abbottabad

Kyelang

AND

NORTH

Taxila Rawalpindi

Srinagar

KASHMIR

Jhelum

AFGHANISTAN

WEST

Sialkot

Jammu Pathankot

Kanga

FRONTIER

Pasrur

Sargodha

Kyelang

I R A N

Lahore

Amritsar

Zahedan

Quetta

PUNJAB

Jullundur

Simla

Chandigarh

Ludhiana

Mussoori

STAN

Montgomery

Ferozepur

Moga Patiala

Ambala

Dehra-Dun

BALUCHI-

Harappa

PUNJAB

Saharanpur

Roorkee

Hardwar

Multan

Nalni

KALAT

Kalat

Hissar

Meerut

New Delhi

KHARAN

BAHAWALPUR

Ghaziabad

Bikaner

Aligarh Budaun

MAKRAN

Turbat

Mohenjo-Daro

KHAIRPUR

Mathura

U

Agra

Gwalior

Bela

Tilaunia

Jaipur

L'ASBELA

Hyderabad

Jodhpur

Ajmer

RAJASTHAN

Jhans

Karachi

Mouths of the Indus

SIND

Chitor

Lalitpur

OMAN

KUTCH

Udaipur

Neemuch

Damoh

Bhuj

Sitamau

Kharua

Banswara

Amkhot

Rutlam

Ujjain

Bhopal

Jab

Rajkot

Nadiad

Godhra

Dhar Indore

BHOPAL

SAURASHTRA

Ahmedabad

Rasalpura

Baroda

Mandleshwar

Mhow

Narbada

Harda

MA

Dholla

Barwani

Khandwa

JUNAGADH

Anklesvar

Anjangaon

Surat

PR

Bulsar

Nasik

Puntamba

Yeotmal

Sanjan

Vadala

Bombay

Ahmednagar

Godavari

HYDERAB

Talegaon

Poona

BOMBAY

Bidar

Hanamcon

A R A B I A N

Sholapur

Secunderabad

Hydera

Ratnagiri

Miri

Vikarabad

Mahbubnagar

Kolhapur

Raichur

Yadgiri

S E A

Vengurla

Belgaum

Kurnool

Gulbarga

GOA

ANDHRA

Cuddapah

Madanapale

Pungalur

MYSORE

Bangalore

Kolar

K

LACCADIVE IS.

Mangalore

Mysore

Bangarapet

Ambur

Mercara

COORG

Muttathur

Calicut

Coonoor

MADRAS

Coimbatore

Trichinopoly

Tanj

Cochin

Kodaikanal

Madurai

TRAVANCORE

Pasumalai

Manamadu

COCHIN

Kottayam

Quilon Palamcottah

Trivandrum

Tinnevelly Neyyoor

Nagercoil CAPE COMORIN

MALDIVE IS.